ANIMALS

Emma Adams

ANIMALS

OBERON BOOKS
LONDON

WWW.OBERONBOOKS.COM

First published in 2015 by Oberon Books Ltd
521 Caledonian Road, London N7 9RH
Tel: +44 (0) 20 7607 3637 / Fax: +44 (0) 20 7607 3629
e-mail: info@oberonbooks.com
www.oberonbooks.com

A catalogue record for this book is available from the British
Library.

PB ISBN: 9781783198801
E ISBN: 9781783198818

Cover design by Flavia Fraser-Cannon

Visit www.oberonbooks.com to read more about all our books
and to buy them. You will also find features, author interviews and
news of any author events, and you can sign up for e-newsletters
so that you're always first to hear about our new releases.

'Sentimentality is the superstructure erected upon brutality.'
Carl Jung, *Ulyssess: A Monologue* (1932)

Animals was developed and produced by Theatre503
and received its world premiere at Theatre503 on Wed 8th April 2015.

CREATIVE TEAM

Lisa Cagnacci – Director

Max Dorey – Designer

Johanna Town – Lighting Designer

Max Pappenheim – Sound Designer

Composer – Timon Wapenaar

Production Manager – Heather Doole

Costume Supervisor – Holly Henshaw

Stage Manager – Benedict Jones

Casting Director – Matthew Dewsbury

Assistant Director – Claire Mullane

Fight Direction – RC-Annie

Associate Lighting Designer – Matt Leventhall

Video Graphic Designer – Katherine Murray-Clark

Marketing Graphic Design – Flavia Fraser-Cannon

Production PR – Chloe Nelkin Consulting

With many thanks to the Royal Victoria Hall Foundation,
Lorraine Williams and all at Wandsworth Life Long Learning,
Mercers Charitable Trust, Alex Rogerson and Arts Council England,
Flavia Fraser-Cannon, Chris Smyrnios and Southwark Playhouse,
Robert Gershinson, Meg and the KI Agency, Theatre Delicatessen,
Wandsworth Council, Hugo and all at The Latchmere, everyone who
donated to the Justgiving campaign, Hampstead Theatre, Orange Tree
Theatre, Caius House, Sarah Dickenson, Chris Campbell, Deirdra
Morris, Jennie Lathan, Alice McCarthy, Grace Chilton, Lachlan
McCall, Measom Freer, and HSC Online, Katherine Low Settlement,
Brian Mullin, Tom Latter, Lauretta Barrow, Clarisse O'Dell,
Philip and Chris Carne and many more who helped bring
this production to the stage.

CAST

MARLENE SIDAWAY (NORMA)

Marlene began her career with Theatre Centre, before going to East 15 Acting School. Her training continued in Repertory Theatres all over the country.

Recent theatre credits include: *The Crucible* and *Enjoy* (West Yorkshire Playhouse); *Macbeth* and *The Daughter in Law* (Sheffield Crucible); *Uncle Vanya* (The Print Room); *The Enchantment* and *A Prayer for Owen Meany* (National Theatre); *Lady in the Van* (Salisbury Playhouse).

Recent television & film credits include: *Wallander* (Bank Pictures); *Hustle* (Kudos); *Me and Orson Welles* (Richard Linklater); *Sensitive Skin* (Baby Cow); *Foyle's War* and *Midsomer Murders* (Bentley Productions); *Doctors* (BBC).

Marlene has also written and performed several one-woman plays and has worked for over 40 years in radio. Most notably, she played Miss Lewis in *King Street Junior* for 100 episodes. In addition, she has recorded over 50 audio books.

SADIE SHIMMIN (JOY)

For Theatre503: *Cold Hands; The Tin Horizon*. Other recent theatre credits include: *Life of Galileo* (Birmingham Rep); *Boris Gudunov/The Life of Galileo* (RSC); *Mary Shelley* (West Yorkshire Playhouse & Tricycle Theatre); *Night Mother* (Old Red Lion Theatre); *You Can't Take It With You* (Southwark Playhouse); *The Rose Tattoo* (National Theatre); *A Voyage Round My Father* (Donmar Warehouse & Wyndhams Theatre); *The Crucible* (Sheffield Crucible), *Life After Life* (National Theatre).

Television credits include: *Eastenders* (BBC); *Mr Selfridge* (ITV); *Silk* (BBC); *Whitechapel* (Carnival Films); *Holby City* and *Upstairs Downstairs* (BBC); *The Nativity* (Red Planet Prods/Kudos for BBC); *Wallander* (BBC/Yellowbird/Left Bank Films); *Coronation Street* (Granada Television); *Harley Street* (Carnival Films); *The Bill* (Talkback Thames); *Casualty* (BBC). Film credits include: *Off Limits* (First Light Films). Radio credits include: *A Voyage Round My Father* (BBC Radio 4); *All The Young Dudes* (BBC Radio 4).

CARA CHASE (HELEN)

Cara's Theatre credits include: *Life's Work* (Theatre 503); *In Memory of Edgar Lutzen* (Old Red Lion); *The Merry Wives of Windsor* (Globe Theatre - Education); *Uncle Vanya* (Trafalgar Studios – Rehearsed Reading); *Goodbye my Love* (Southwark Playhouse); *Henry V (Extract)* (Rose Theatre); *A Lie of the Mind* (Battersea Arts Centre); *Random Acts of Malice* (Union Theatre); *Tube* (Union Theatre); *Mountain Language* (Royal Court).

Television & film credits include: *Stargirl* (Short Film); *Margaret* (Short Film); *Subject* (Feature Film); *Agatha Christie – A Life in Pictures* (BBC 2); *Island at War* (Granada); *April Rhapsody* (Sinoscope); *Sex, Guys, and Video Tapes* (Channel 4).

Commercials include: Terry's Chocolate Orange, Lloyds Pharmacy, Nationwide, Wales Tourist Board, Millennium Dome.

STEVE HANSELL (NOAH)

Steve's theatre credits include: *Scrooge* (UK Tour); *Blood Brothers* (Phoenix Theatre); *Erpingham Camp* (Hydrocracker for Brighton Festival); *Christmas Carol* (Southwark Playhouse); *Plague Over England* (Duchess Theatre & Finborough Theatre); *How To Disappear Completely And Never Be Found* (Sheffield Crucible & Southwark Playhouse); *Animal Farm* (Peter Hall Company); *Motortown* (Royal Court); *Volpone* (Wilton's Music Hall); *Story Pimp* (Soho Theatre); *Mother Courage And Her Children* (Watford Palace Theatre); *Holy Days* (Soho Theatre).

Television credits include: *Southcliffe; May Day* (Kudos/BBC)*; Injustice* (ITV)*; Law & Order* (Kudos ITV)*; Living with the Infidels; Eastenders, Waking the Dead* and *Desperados* (BBC)*; The Bill* (Talkback Thames Television)*; The Friday Night Project* (Princess Television).

MILLY THOMAS (MAYA)

Milly trained as an actor at The Royal Central School of Speech and Drama.

Theatre credits include: *A First World Problem* (Theatre503); *Seeing Double: Vision & Seeing Double: Figures* (Edinburgh Fringe); *Coram Boy* (The Pleasance Theatre - Islington); *After the War* (Cambridge ADC) – Winner IUDF Award; *Playhouse Creatures* (Windsor Studio – Bristol); *Twelfth Night* (Edinburgh Fringe).

Television credits include: *X Company* (Temple Street Productions/CBC); *Doctors* (BBC).

Film credits include: *And Then I Was French* (Dog Eared Films); *Woman in Gold* (The Weinstein Company/BBC Films); *Hearts and Minds* (Scratchmark Films).

EMMA ADAMS – WRITER

Emma writes for theatre spaces, unusual places, and screens. Her writing is often fantastical and surreal, ranging from dark political satire for adults through to adventure comedy for children. National tours include: *Home Sweet Home* (Freedom Studios), a magic-realist, multi-sensory, immersive theatre experience for older audiences, gaining 4 Stars from the *Guardian*; *Forgotten Things* (Red Ladder), shortlisted for the Meyer-Whitworth Award; *Ugly* (Red Ladder), published by Oberon Books. Other work includes: *Northern Big Board* (Chol /Slung Low), a site-specific adventure for families at Shipley Pool; *Freakoid* (Ovalhouse), a one-woman, sci-fi, queer-future, who-dun-it (nominated for an Off West End Theatre Award); *Brimming* (Dep Arts), part of The Enough Project, a surreal, dark comedy about surviving emotional abuse; *Fix This* (Space2), based on research with teenagers and parents living with self-harm, touring to schools in the North. Emma was Writer in Residence during West Yorkshire Playhouse's New Writing Season 2012, attended The Royal Court invitation group 2013 and was selected for Accelerate – the Lowry/Jerwood Programme for Artistic Development 2013/14. When not writing Emma lectures part-time at Northern Film School.

LISA CAGNACCI – DIRECTOR

Lisa Cagnacci is Associate Artistic Director at Theatre503, where she has directed *Dog Days, Billy Chickens Is A Psychopath Superstar* (Theatre503/Latitude), *Confessional* (Theatre503/ALRA) and several short plays including work by Steve Waters, Jon Brittain, Brad Birch, Dominic Cavendish, Gemma Langford and Melissa Bubnic. She was previously an associate at Southwark Playhouse, where she wrote and directed the 2010 Christmas show *Anansi: An African Fairy Tale.* Other directing includes *Hannah_27: Valiant Adventures in Online Dating* (Made From Scratch/ Latitude), *Blood Wedding* (Broadway Theatre, Barking), *Cuban Charm* (Rosemary Branch), *Losing Unity* (C Venues and tour), *How To Be Female* (Pleasance), *Playing* (ClubWest, Edinburgh and tour), *Vita & Virginia* (White Bear).

MAX DOREY – DESIGNER

Max graduated from the Professional Theatre Design MA at Bristol Old Vic Theatre School in 2012. He was a finalist for the Linbury Prize in 2013 and was a trainee/ assistant designer at the RSC in 2013/14.

Theatre credits include: *Lardo* (Old Red Lion); *Coolatully* (Finborough Theatre); *Sleight and Hand* (Edinburgh Fringe); *I Can Hear You, This is Not an Exit* (The Other Place at the Courtyard, RSC/Royal Court Upstairs); *Count Ory* (Blackheath Halls); *Black Jesus* (Finborough Theatre); *The Duke in Darkness* (Tabard Theatre).

Max was nominated for an OffWestEnd Award in 2012 for Best Set Design.

JOHANNA TOWN – LIGHTING DESIGNER

Johanna is an Associate Artist for Theatre503. Her credits include *The Life of Stuff*, which received an Offie nomination for 'Best Lighting Designer'.

Johanna has designed the lighting for numerous major theatre companies both in the UK and internationally including The National Theatre, RSC, West Yorkshire Playhouse, Sheffield Theatres, Royal Exchange Manchester and Traverse Theatre. She has designed over fifty productions for the Royal Court Theatre in London, where she was Head of Lighting for 17 years. She has enjoyed a long collaboration with Out of Joint, under the directorship of Max Stafford-Clark.

She has lit many Opera productions for Scottish Opera, Trinity College Opera, Classical Opera Company, Nice Opera House, Estonia National Opera and has recently lit *Porgy & Bess* for the Danish Opera House.

Johanna is also the Professional Rep for the Association of Lighting Designers.

MAX PAPPENHEIM – SOUND DESIGNER

Max's theatre credits include: *Toast, The Man Who Shot Liberty Valance, The Archimedes Principle* (Park Theatre); *Wink* (Theatre503); *CommonWealth* (Almeida Theatre); *Little Light, The Distance* (Orange Tree Theatre, Richmond); *Ghost, Strangers On A Train* (English Theatre, Frankfurt); *Usagi Yojimbo, Johnny Got His Gun, Three Sisters, Fiji Land, Our Ajax* (Southwark Playhouse); *Mrs Lowry and Son* (Trafalgar Studios); *Coolatully, Rachel, Martine, Variation on a Theme, Black Jesus, Somersaults, The Soft of Her Palm, The Fear of Breathing* (Finborough Theatre); *The Faction's Rep Season 2015* (New Diorama Theatre); *Giovanni* (Silent Opera); *Being Tommy Cooper* (National Tour); *Shipwrecked!, Irma Vep, Kafka v Kafka* (Brockley Jack); *Freefall* (New Wimbledon Theatre Studio); *Awkward Conversations with Animals I've F*cked* (Underbelly, Edinburgh); *Below the Belt* (Pleasance, Edinburgh). As an associate: *The Island* (Young Vic); *Fleabag* (Soho Theatre). Max has been nominated for OffWestEnd Awards in 2012, 2014 and 2015 for Best Sound Designer.

HEATHER DOOLE – PRODUCTION MANAGER

Heather is a freelance production manager. Recent projects include *State Red*, *Elephants* and *Deposit* at the Hampstead Theatre; *Albert Herring* at Upstairs at the Gatehouse; *Cinderella and the Beanstalk* at Theatre503; *Radiant Vermin* at the Tobacco Factory Theatre, Bristol, and the Soho Theatre, London; the *Women Centre Stage* festival at the National Theatre and assisting on *Bull* at the Young Vic Theatre.

BENEDICT JONES - STAGE MANAGER

Benedict Jones trained at the Bristol Old Vic Theatre School in Stage Management, graduating in 2013. He is a Stage Manager, working in theatres across the country and is also Production Manager for the physical theatre company *Blue Crate Theatre*. Theatre credits include; Company Stage Manager for *Faust* (National Tour). Stage and Technical Manager for *Close to You* (Southwark Playhouse and Brighton Fringe) and *Three Witches* (Belgrade Theatre). Stage Manager for the theatre/circus spectacular *Walking The Chains* (The Passenger Shed, Bristol); *Stardust* (South West Tour); the *GB Theatre Open-Air Shakespeare Tour 2014* (Macbeth & The Comedy of Errors, Nationwide); *Spokesong* (Finborough Theatre); *Oedipus Retold* (Tristan Bates Theatre); *Starry Night - A Nativity Play* (Bristol Schools Tour); *Moonfleet* (West Country Tour); *Surrealissimo* (Alma Tavern Theatre); *Mr Kolpert* (Alma Tavern Theatre). Assistant Stage Manager for *Dancing At Lughnasa* (Tobacco Factory Theatre).

MATTHEW DEWSBURY - CASTING DIRECTOR

Matthew is the Casting Assistant at the Royal Shakespeare Company. Prior to that he was the Casting and Producing Assistant at The Watermill Theatre. His credits as Casting Director include: *A Mad World, My Masters*, (RSC/ETT); *A Handful of Stars*, (Theatre503 and Trafalgar Studios, West End Transfer); Theatre 503; *Much Ado About Nothing*, Reading Between the Lines; *Ragnorak*, Eastern Angles; *Glamping (Now I am Running Stag)*, Windswept productions (workshop).

CLAIRE MULLANE - ASSISTANT DIRECTOR

Claire's directing credits include *Nineteen* (Rapid Write Response at Theatre503); *Made Up* (Five Minute Festival at the Lost Theatre); *Form 84B* (Writers Bloc at the Old Red Lion) and *The Questionnaire* (Writers Bloc at Canal Cafe Theatre).

MATT LEVENTHALL - ASSOCIATE LIGHTING DESIGNER

After serving as president of the University of Nottingham New Theatre, Matt trained at the Royal Academy of Dramatic Art, graduating top of his class. Matt recently returned to RADA to take up post as Assistant Head of Lighting.

Recent Theatre/Opera includes: *A Christmas Carol* (Old Red Lion); *Sikes and Nancy*, (UK Tour and Trafalgar Studios December 2014); *Light* (Barbican and European Tour, for LIMF and Theatre Ad Infinitum); *Mrs Warren's Profession* (John Gielgud Theatre); *Suffolk Stories* (Theatre Royal, Bury St Emunds for Lubkinfinds); *God's Own Country* (UK Tour for Fine Mess Theatre); *Bear* (Old Red Lion); *Who Framed Roger Rabbit?* (Secret Cinema, The Troxy); *Random* (John Gielgud Theatre); *Fishskin Trousers* (Finborough Theatre) ** Offie Finalist – Best Lighting Designer; *Hamlet* (St Mary's Theatre, Nottingham); *Bedbound* (Trinity Theatre, Kent); *The Infant* (Vivien Cox Theatre, Guildford); *Bed* (Nottingham Lakeside); *Madame Butterfly* (Leatherhead Theatre).

Matt is also a regular visiting artist at LAMDA, designs include: *Have a Nice Life; Women of Troy; But Not As We Know It; The Walworth Farce; Joseph K; The Cagebirds; Land Without Words*.

THEATRE503 IS THE AWARD-WINNING HOME OF GROUNDBREAKING PLAYS

Led by Artistic Director Paul Robinson, Theatre503 is a flagship fringe venue committed to producing new work that is game-changing, relevant, theatrical and surprising. We are the smallest theatre to win and an Olivier award and we offer more opportunities to new writers than anywhere in the UK.

THEATRE503 TEAM
Artistic Director – Paul Robinson
Executive Director – Jeremy Woodhouse
Producer and Head of Marketing – Polly Ingham
Associate Artistic Director – Lisa Cagnacci
Office Manager – Emily Hubert
Literary Manager – Steve Harper
Literary Coordinators – Lauretta Barrow, Tom Latter
Resident Assistant Producers – Franky Green, Liam Harrison
Volunteer Coordinators – Serafina Cusack, Simon Mander
'Young Creative Leaders' Project Manager – Louise Abbots
Senior Readers - Kate Brower, Karis Halsall, Clare O'Hara,
Jimmy Osbourne, Imogen Sarre
Associate Directors - Gemma Fairlie, Tom Littler
503 Five Resident Writers - Ella Greenhill, Brian Mullin,
Neasa O'Callaghan, Vinay Patel, Chloe Todd-Fordham

THEATRE503 BOARD

Erica Whyman (Chair), Dennis Kelly, Royce Bell, Peter Benson, Chris Campbell, Kay Ellen Consolver, Ben Hall, Marcus Markou, Geraldine Sharpe-Newton, Jack Tilbury, Eleanor Lloyd, Roy Williams.

And we couldn't do what we do without out brilliant volunteers:

Annabel Pemberton, Nuno Faisca, Rosie Akerman, Diyan Zora, Tobias Chapple, Joseph Ackerman, Alexandra Coyne, Anuska Zaremba-Pike, Cecilia Segar, Valeria Bello, Larner Taylor, Damian Robertson, Jumoke, Valeria Carboni, Mike Bale, Serafina Cusack, Louise Fairbrother, Caroline Jowett, Jim Mannering, Oluwafuntu Ojumu, Imogen Robertson, Chidimma Chukwu, Jill Segal, Elena Valentine, Tess Hardy, Kenneth Hawes, Anna Gorajek, Maya Kirtley.

THEATRE503 IS SUPPORTED BY:

Philip and Chris Carne, Angela Hyde-Courtney and the Audience Club, Kay Ellen Consolver, Cas Donald, Edna Kissman, Eileen Glynn, Deborah Shaw and Steve Marqhardt, Marisa Drew, Jerwood/Ponsonby, Andrew and Julia Johnson, Georgia Oetker, Stuart Mullins, Michael Morfey, Geraldine Sharpe-Newton, Penny Egan, Liz Padmore, Bernice Chitnis, Lisa Forrell, Abigail Thaw, Charlotte Westenra, Frankie Sangwin, Mike and Hilary Tyler, Sue and Keith Hamilton, Sandra Chalmers, David Chapman and Judy Molloy, Georgie Grant Haworth, Amy Rotherham, Kate Beswick, Craig Simpson, Jason Meiniger, Yve Newbold, Juliana Breitenbach.

THEATRE503, 503 BATTERSEA PARK RD, LONDON, SW11 3BW
020 7978 7040 | WWW.THEATRE503.COM
@THEATRE503 | FACEBOOK.COM/THEATRE503

SHINE A LIGHT ON THEATRE503...

Theatre503 receives no public subsidy as a venue and we cannot survive without the transformative support of our friends. For as little as £23 a year you can help us remain 'Arguably the most important theatre in Britain today' *(Guardian)*

Becoming a Friend of Theatre503 is simple.

Annual Support donations are invited in five tiers:

FOOTLIGHT - £23

- Priority notice of productions and events
- Priority booking for all productions
- Special ticket offers
- E-mail bulletins

SPOTLIGHT - £53

As Footlight plus

- Access to sold-out shows
- Credit in the theatre foyer, play texts, and on the website

LIMELIGHT - £173

As Spotlight plus

- Two complimentary tickets to Theatre503's hottest new play each year
- Complimentary tickets to play readings and other one-off supporter events
- Free programmes
- Ticket exchange service for pre-booked tickets (with 24 hours notice)

HIGHLIGHT - £503

As Limelight plus

- Two complimentary tickets for each Theatre503 in house production
- Opportunities to attend rehearsals
- Invitation to annual high level supporters' party hosted by the Artistic Director

STARLIGHT - £1003

- A bespoke package enables our Starlight to engage with Theatre503's work as they wish. This can include bespoke entertaining opportunities at the theatre, invitations to attend supper parties with the Artistic Director, or closer engagement with playwrights and the artistic team. Starlights can also choose a strand of Theatre503's work to support, for example a particular production, funding Theatre503 writing programmes or work in the local community. Please visit our website theatre503.com for details on specific appeals also.

One off donations also make an enormous difference to the way Theatre503 is able to operate. Whether you are able to give £10 or £1000 your gift will help us continue to create work of award-winning standard.

To become a member or make a one off donation email your interest to: info@ theatre503.com, or by post to: Theatre503, The Latchmere, 503 Battersea Park Road, London, SW11 3BW.

Alternatively visit our website theatre503.com or ring 020 7978 7040 to sign up for membership directly.

If you are a UK tax payer and able to make a gift aid donation please let us know as we receive 25p per pound more on top of your donation in government grant.

Characters

NORMA PRATT

77, Any ethnicity. A retired nurse, frail, with poor mobility. Norma no longer goes out, but she rules her little kingdom with an iron fist. She takes great pride in her quick intellect. She may not be as clever or objective as she likes to think.

JOY

59, Any ethnicity. Norma's live-in home-help / cleaner. Widowed and childless. Is facing an uncertain future but tries to meet the day with a smile. Always moving, always talking, always watching. She means well. She is smarter than she pretends.

HELEN CANNING

70, Any ethnicity. Helen is healthy and excellent at crosswords. She moved in next door 15 years ago, so by Norma's standards is still an unwelcome incomer. Outwardly sunny, she is far more pragmatic then even she suspects as yet.

MAYA

17, Any ethnicity. A day away from her 18th birthday Maya is sweet but spoilt and willful. Despite attending therapy sessions to avert thought, she finds she just can't stop thinking. She is innocent enough to truly believe that knowledge will set her free.

NOAH

35, Any ethnicity. A doting dad and newly promoted inspector within the Utility Force. He believes in doing what needs to be done, regardless of what that is, because everything he does is for Maya. She must merit. Everything depends on it.

NOTE ON LINES

/ = An overlap and/or an invitation for the next actor to smash in with their next line.

… = A pause in the action, a search for words or the loss of words.

THE SETTING

An estate of bungalows, on the edge of a once respectable market town in North Yorkshire. First impressions suggest the present, but it's 2046 (16 years after residents first awoke to find the 'sea arrived', changing the town overnight into a seaside resort).

LOCATIONS

The locations coexist allowing for seamless and/or simultaneous action.

A Living Room with a doorway leading to an unseen Kitchen / Front Door on one side.

On the other side of the Living Room there is a doorway leading to a Hall.

The Hall has bedroom doors, a Steel Door and a Back Door leading to the Garden.

The Garden has a Fence / Gate leading to an unseen Drive.

The Sky.

Streets.

ACT ONE

SCENE 1 – LIVING ROOM – MID MORNING

Scuffed, bare, yet clean. Sunshine leaks in through closed curtains. A RECLINER with an antimacassar dwarfs two stools, a table, newspaper piles and reference books.

JOY, keys at her hip, in skirt, tabard and slippers, scurries in from the Kitchen, dragging polythene bags full of bread crusts and broken biscuits… She watches the Hall door for an anxious moment… Then suddenly slumps down on the recliner, grabbing a biscuit, popping the leg support, and lying back to guiltily, greedily chew…

The SOUND of a toilet flushing (off).

NORMA: *(Off.)* JOY!

> *JOY leaps from the chair, wipes crumbs from her mouth and runs toward the Hall door. Then stops. Runs back to the recliner and pulls the antimacassar straight. Just as…*
>
> *NORMA, supported by a stick, in neck and wrist braces (held together with gaffer tape) and wearing a worn but distinguished frock, struggles in through the Hall door.*

NORMA: I called! Where were you?

JOY: In the kitchen. Answering the door… Mr Brown dropped off the treasure and /

NORMA: About time! Tardy little man, turning up whenever he likes. He forgets I made him. Did you check the bags? They look light to me. I've told you! We have to watch Mr Brown!

JOY: No… I mean. Yes! I know. I watch everyone! But I didn't check them yet / because

NORMA: What's wrong?.. You're not coming down with something?

JOY: No… But… Norma! I think… I need to talk to you… I think you should sit down.

17

NORMA moves toward the recliner. But then stops dead.

NORMA: The antimacassar has been straightened… But I distinctly remember leaving it creased.

JOY opens her mouth. But no words come.

NORMA: 'Did you sit in my chair again, Joy? Why? What have I told you! /

JOY: It may look robust, but the chair is now out of warranty.' /

NORMA: And any chair with a recliner mechanism, even a quality one, has a / shelf life.

JOY: Shelf life. /

NORMA: But this is not just any old chair! Is it? It is the last link I have to dear Graham. He picked it out just days before he was swept away… Every time you sit in it, you bring the day I must lose him all over again a terrible moment closer. Is that what you want?

JOY: No Norma.

NORMA: No Norma! So keep off! Because if you can't there are other people who will!

JOY: Other people?

NORMA: Professional people who would give anything for a job and a little wooden stool to sit on.

JOY: Professionals are Incomers! Settling here with their fresh green permits and their aromatherapy skills! Stealing all my work when I've only got one legal year left in me.

NORMA: Nonsense! There are still some local professionals to be found.

JOY: They might struggle with your 'difficult tasks' though… You said I was indi-pensable!

NORMA: It's indi-spensable! And I may have… But you haven't provided a windfall in months. And I have mouths to feed. You seem to forget that. So maybe I should get someone new.

JOY: But, this is my home. There's only one spare room
and I won't share it with an Incomer /

NORMA: Joy? If I hired someone new, you wouldn't need to
share the room because you would be sacked… I would have
sacked you. You understand? It means you would have to
leave. /

JOY: And who would carry the keys then? You haven't thought
any of this through… Please! Just sit down and listen. I have
news! It's fresh off the vine / and

NORMA: How dare you! A woman in my position must think
everything through, Joy! Everything!

JOY: I didn't mean /

NORMA: I may well be officially useless and on the wrong side of
the law, but I am not stupid!

> *NORMA sinks into the recliner, snaps up a newspaper
> (revealing half its words are cut out) and tries to read it but
> she's too cross. She snaps it back down.*

NORMA: *(Cont'd.)* I run this estate, so don't try and tell me I can't
run my own household. I could get a new home help, like
that!
I would simply demand verifiable, fully local references / and

JOY: 'Local references' she says! You don't know what it's like out
there now! Incomers swarming all over, come to admire the
sea in their soft shoes and animal print sweaters! /

NORMA: I know about Incomers!

JOY: You don't! Everyday it's worse. I didn't dare tell you about
what happened at the post office.

NORMA: Yesterday gone? Did Postmaster Hanson give you
trouble?

JOY: No. I gave him a lovely hand job and he slipped me the
picture stamps just as he always does. He is very local and a
perfect gentleman /

NORMA: I wish you wouldn't grow fond of the men we blackmail.

JOY: But he's very clean down below. I can't say that for most of the men I see to for you /

NORMA: Just get to the point. /

JOY: They were outside the post office. A family of Incomers. Mother, fragrant, bubble-wrapping the little ones nicely. Father ever so prime, like a lion, patting the arm of Grandma, who's milking it. You've never seen such a well lifted face! She was a pro!

NORMA: Lucky little bitch! What I could do with an opportunity like that. /

JOY: Father must be loaded! Grandma's sentimental attachment fee alone is enough. But I never saw such well adjusted children, and we all know, a good therapist doesn't come cheap /

NORMA: The future those children will merit. It makes / you sick!

JOY: You sick! But there's more… After they finish swanning around with their ice cream /

NORMA: Grandma got a bloody ice cream too? /

JOY: I told you she was a pro. After they finish, yes? And Mother's wiped everyone's sticky hands? That's when Father herds them all into a car. But it's not his car. It's Mrs Cooke's!

NORMA: You're sure?

JOY: I followed them. I saw. They've got her dog, her house and her car. All polished up with nice new green number plates… So what do you think about your 'local references' now?

NORMA: These people! They promised us life boats when the tsunami hit. Did we ever see them?

JOY: No Norma!

NORMA: No. They sent a floating barge, called it a promenade, banned words like 'flooding' and 'hey presto'. We get

swamped by idiots, desperate to move to an affordable
'seaside resort'.

JOY: Its an insult to all of our drowned.

NORMA: *(Shouting.)* If dear Graham had lived he would never
have stood for this!

JOY: *(Whispering.)* I know, I do… But you mustn't shout.
It isn't safe.

> *And now JOY's face begins to crumple.*

NORMA: You're hypoglycemic again Joy! Put your head between
your knees and have a biscuit.

JOY: No. I won't thank you… I'll be alright.

NORMA: You've been on half rations all week. It makes you
unbearable. Have one. Really, I insist.

> *JOY guiltily looks at NORMA, then shakes her head.*

NORMA: *(Cont'd.)* Did you sit in my chair and help yourself to the
treasure too? Oh Joy! How could you?

JOY: I was upset. I've been trying to tell you but you won't listen.
You're not safe any more /

NORMA: Ridiculous! Who says I'm not safe?

JOY: Mrs Khan? You know? Oh you do! Does the tasteful
pornography… She was in her darkroom, exposing prints
after a session with a Utility Inspector. Yes? When she sees his
paperwork, caught in frame… So, she enlarges it /

NORMA: I have always had a soft spot for Mrs Khan. Very bright.
What did the paperwork say? /

JOY: Sadly a lot was lost behind his cock in the foreground. But
she could make out something about Incomers needing more
space. And an order. Everyone with an outstanding estimate
must be visited and retested within the next two weeks.

NORMA: You saw this photograph?

JOY: Well, no. Mr Brown told me about it, when he dropped off the treasure. But he says it's all over the vine, so it must be true… What will we do if they come to check your estimate?

NORMA: Hearsay, gossip and supposition.

JOY: But what happened to poor Mrs Cooke proves it. The Utility must be cracking down.

NORMA: I have the best forged amber permit on this estate and thanks to your legendary skills, I have Inspector Stevens in my pocket. He won't rock the boat. Everything will be fine.

JOY: You're wrong! If poor Mrs Cooke can be cleared, so can you. You must see that?

A silent glare hangs between JOY and NORMA.

NORMA: No. But I'll tell you what I do see. I see a home-help chattering away, trying to avoid doing her chores… Have you even started the sandwich packs yet?

JOY: No Norma.

NORMA: Well why on earth not? The Sandwich Circle has not had a crumb from us in over a week!

JOY: But, Norma. You sacked me.

NORMA: I did not. I was being hypothetical. I merely said it's possible that I could, if I wanted to.

> *JOY beams. NORMA, seeing this, angrily pulls her chair lever and her legs fly out.*

NORMA: *(Cont'd.)* Oh stop grinning like a lunatic. The Sandwich Circle must have meat Joy. Get on!

JOY: Yes Norma.

JOY exits out of the Hall door.

SCENE 2 – STREET – MID MORNING

The SOUND of two van doors being shut.

NOAH in a UTILITY uniform (part police, part plumber) enters, carrying a tool bag. MAYA follows on, in a skater helmet and overcoat made from bubble-wrap. Underneath she has rainbow knee and elbow pads, a pink T-shirt, shorts and pumps. She carries a pink rucksack.

NOAH stops, unfurls a map. MAYA kicks at her heels.

NOAH: We're almost having a really great time aren't we?

MAYA: Yes.

NOAH: And Daddy's work is important and means Daddy can afford to buy the things you like.

MAYA: But not a fun-day-memory-package like Maddy O'Brien's Daddy is buying for her.

NOAH: Because Daddy enjoys a zero hour contract, we decided it would be much more fun for us to spend the day together instead of getting a boring old memory-package. Remember?

    MAYA shrugs.

NOAH: And it's not Daddy's fault that work doubled his targets on the second most important day of your life. Is it?

MAYA: Uh-huh.

NOAH: Don't 'Uh-huh' Maya! It makes it sound like you've got breathing problems.

MAYA: I'm sorry.

NOAH: I mean it. You mustn't say 'Uh-huh' tomorrow during your birthday test. OK?

MAYA: OK Daddy. I'm sorry I'm so stupid. I don't know why I always get things wrong.

NOAH: Don't be silly. You're not always wrong. What does Dr Hardy say about worrying?

MAYA: 'Worrying is wrong. Stop it and do nice things'.

NOAH: 'Stop it and do nice things'… I pay a lot for Dr Hardy, so please do as he says.

MAYA: I'm trying. But it's hard. When is our fun-day ever going to start being fun, Daddy?

NOAH: Soon.

MAYA: OK… Because… I have to have some fun to talk about in my birthday test tomorrow. That's the whole point of today. You know that. If I don't have fun soon I might not merit.

NOAH: Of course you'll merit. Darling! Look at me… This is just pre-fun. So you'll be fine.

MAYA: Pre-fun. What is pre-fun?

NOAH: Well… it's the bit where you imagine the balloon I'm going to get for you later.

MAYA: A balloon? I love balloons! Can I have it now?

NOAH: No. You'll get it at two, when I finish the estimates and our fun-day-proper begins. OK?

MAYA: Will it be a meteorological balloon? Is it huge? It is isn't it! Me and Ling May did experiments with balloons! We sent them up up up to measure atmospheric pressure / and

NOAH: *(Whispering.)* Maya. No. What have I said to you about using banned weather words?

MAYA: Uh… Stop it or it could get Daddy sacked?

NOAH: That's right. So. Try again… What kind of legal balloon would Daddy get for his Maya?

MAYA: Is it pretty, totally awesome and pink?

NOAH: Yes. Good girl. That's right. Your balloon is going to be totally awesome and pink.

MAYA: Thanks Daddy.

NOAH: So now you imagine that and I'll read my map. Deal?

> *MAYA scrunches her eyes up… And then opens them.*

MAYA: Daddy? I'm trying to think about the pink balloon but Ling May keeps popping up inside my head. Would it be OK to think about Ling May with the pink balloon?

NOAH: Ling May did not deserve our fun time, green permit lifestyle, smiles or use of Daddy's van. She got careless, talked to you about things you should never know and /

MAYA: Sally Bishop says Ling May was baking a bun in her oven for you but you didn't want it. Why didn't you like Ling May's baking?

NOAH: That isn't true… It's not! She didn't bake a bun I didn't want. I promise.

MAYA: I miss her Daddy. Everyday. I know I shouldn't. But I do.

NOAH: Well you have to stop it. Ling May was only ever a Comfort Girl. That's all. Once you turn 18 I'll explain everything and then you'll understand.

MAYA: Once I'm 18. Not yet. Why not yet? I'm 18 tomorrow and it's stupid, stupid, stupid to wait.

NOAH: Lovely, it's not stupid, it's the law. So come on, think about the pink balloon.

MAYA shuts her eyes and screws her face up 'imagining'.

NOAH: *(Cont'd.)* Because we're going to make the best fun memories playing with it later.

MAYA: You're sure?

NOAH: My diminished years depend on it. But we'll talk about that when we sign the paperwork.

MAYA: I can't wait! Will we colour the paperwork in? Will I sign with a pencil or pen?

NOAH: You know this. You'll find out everything after you've merited tomorrow, won't you.

NOAH returns to his map, starts making notes.

MAYA: Not if I work it out for myself first? Like… I worked out burning means 'firm chat'.

NOAH: Who talked to you about burning? That is not a nice word. It's a bad word!

MAYA: In the playground. Jackie Harris says everyone knows you burnt Ling May. But you told me she left because you had a 'firm chat'. So does that mean you burnt Mummy too? I don't mind. I don't miss her. I miss Ling May.

NOAH: *(Shouting.)* For God's sake! Why can't you just stop fucking thinking about Ling May!

A mortified silence.

MAYA: You said fucking, Daddy. You are so rubbish at remembering not to say it. Dr Hardy says it's really important that you try /

NOAH: I know, I'm sorry. Listen to me… Burning and the cross F word, that just slipped out of Daddy's mouth by accident, because he's very tired? /

MAYA: The cross F word? You mean fucking?

NOAH: Yes. Stop saying it. Both words are something that grown-ups sometimes say, but little girls never do. Ever. You understand? You have to forget them. Will you do that for me?

MAYA: It's OK. Dr Hardy helped me make a little box in my mind where I lock away all my sad, horrid, non fun thoughts. Would you like me to put burning and fucking in there too?

NOAH: Yes please. Look… I was going to save it but I think you should have the balloon now.

NOAH opens his bag and pulls a pink balloon out.

MAYA: Thank you, Daddy. You are totally brilliant. You always make sad things better.

NOAH kisses MAYA, gives her the balloon and his van keys.

NOAH: OK. So, take the balloon to the cab of the van. Don't go in the back. Don't touch the handbrake. Don't touch the radio. Don't stand on the seats, and make sure you / have?

MAYA: Have total brilliant fun.

NOAH: That's a golden rule. You remember that.

> *NOAH kisses MAYA and exits.*

SCENE 3 – LIVING ROOM – MID MORNING

NORMA sits in the recliner, musing on a crossword.

NORMA: *(Shouting.)* Joy! Have you finished yet? I don't want
Helen seeing that we've fallen behind.

> *JOY enters from the Hall with a pile of nasty carved ham.*

JOY: Helen wouldn't judge. She's too lovely.

> *JOY sits on a stool and starts slapping the ham between crusts
> of moulding bread from the 'treasure bags'.*

JOY: I don't know why she upsets you so much. You'd like her if
you got to know her.

NORMA: Helen doesn't upset me.

JOY: Is it because you feel bad about the mix up? /

NORMA: I do not feel bad. We had an awful mix up. But awful
mix ups / happen.

JOY: Happen. Yes. Only. It feels so awful when a mix up happens
to someone as nice as Helen.

NORMA: Oh be honest! She's one of them. /

JOY: No! /

NORMA: You wouldn't speak to her for the first five years after
she moved in.

JOY: Because she was an Incomer to start with, so we had to be
careful… But I watched and intercepted her mail for all of
those years, and I couldn't find a single fault. She's lovely.

NORMA: Voyeur!

JOY: You didn't mind me finding out she owns an uncensored
Chambers Dictionary, did you?

NORMA: Exactly. And that's why we put up with her. She's useful. But she is not our friend.

JOY: You don't mean that. Deep down. I know you don't Norma. I know it.

NORMA waves her crossword at JOY.

NORMA: 28 across, 7 letters 'A tune to esteem?' Do you have the slightest idea how to start to solve that? No! So now we name the problem. Joy doesn't do / crosswords.

JOY: Crosswords. No. I'm more of a practical person. /

NORMA: I have a huge intellectual range, but I can not be expected to know everything. /

JOY: It's not fair to blame me. /

NORMA: But you show no interest in trying to improve. And so I find I must have a partner. /

JOY: I just can't do them. /

NORMA: Well you'd do well to think about it. Because in a years time your precious green permit will be gone, and you'll be stuck in a chair like this. If you can't do crosswords what then?

JOY: I won't ever have a chair as nice as yours.

The SOUND of a door bell.

NORMA: Don't be obtuse. Just answer the bloody door! She'll think I've gone out.

JOY: I doubt that… You haven't been out for seven years.

JOY exits into the Kitchen.

NORMA pretends indifference and studies her crossword intently as the SOUND (off) of a door opening is heard.

JOY: *(Off.)* Helen! We were just saying how much we were looking forward to seeing you. Come in.

JOY and HELEN enter from the Kitchen. HELEN wears a full face balaclava, a jumper with an embroidered unicorn and

> *slacks. She carries a handbag. As she pulls her balaclava off she reveals well dyed hair and a lovely smile.*
>
> *NORMA won't look up from her crossword…*

Norma? Look who it is… Helen's here. Norma?

NORMA: You're early.

HELEN: *(To JOY.)* Am I? I'm sure you said eleven o'clock?

NORMA: Eleven thirty. But never mind. You're here now.

> *HELEN moves further into the room, sees the pile of sandwiches. Looks longingly at them. Tries not to.*

HELEN: And it's lovely to see you, Norma. So good of you to invite me round.

NORMA: The week wouldn't be complete if we didn't see little Helen.

JOY: I'll just be in the kitchen then.

> *JOY takes the pile of sandwiches and exits into the Kitchen.*
>
> *NORMA watches HELEN watching the sandwiches disappear.*

NORMA: Forgot your *Chamber's Dictionary* again?

HELEN: Oh, blast! I put it out but forgot to pick it up.

NORMA: I hope your mind isn't going dear?

HELEN: I'll go back.

NORMA: No. Don't trouble yourself. I'll send Joy.

> *An awkward pause.*

HELEN: Keeping well?

NORMA: Awful. The pain in my joints has kept me awake for the last two nights running.

HELEN: Oh you poor thing. That must be /

NORMA: You look febrile. You're not bringing a cold round for me to catch, are you?

HELEN: I would never do that. I'm just a little hungry dear. A little light headed. But I'm not ill.

NORMA: Some would call that kind of certainty hubris. People are Trojan horses when it comes to disease.

HELEN: Well, perhaps. But really, I feel absolutely fine.

NORMA: Take TB. It can incubate in the hapless carrier for years. If Joy ends up dying, two years hence, like Keats in my arms, who will have egg on her face then?

HELEN: Better years of illness than these awful clearances… Did you hear about poor Mrs Cooke?

NORMA: Of course I heard. It's all very sad.

HELEN: Well, I should imagine Mrs Cooke would have welcomed the chance of a long illness.

NORMA: Only little Helen could make the death sweats of Tuberculosis sound appealing.

HELEN: I don't mean… It's just I would hate not to be able to say my goodbyes.

NORMA: As you've so many to say goodbye to!

HELEN: Yes. I have friends… You. Joy. Mr Brown… There are people.

HELEN begins to tear up.

NORMA: Oh don't! I was merely noting a paradox. Namely that you will insist you are perfectly well, yet you have no medical proof to support your unfounded, complacent outlook.

HELEN: Why do you do this, every week? When you know we can't go to the Doctor anymore.

HELEN searches for a hanky to dab her eyes.

NORMA: You're getting upset over nothing.

HELEN: *(Upset.)* I've been fine since I turned 60. I've had ten years of really good fortune / and

NORMA: Other than your annus horribilis of course.

HELEN: That had nothing to do with my health.

NORMA: I doubt losing the sentimental attachment of a daughter makes one feel well.

HELEN: *(Very upset.)* It's not my fault that you are officially Useless while I am merely Diminished.

NORMA: Here she goes. Crowing about her nice legal amber permit again.

HELEN: For God's sake! Having an amber permit is hardly something to crow about. /

NORMA: Don't you dare say that! I would give… I would give up my chair to have a real amber permit again. I would! When you have to start forging yours, you'll understand.

HELEN: I know… But I can't help being seven years younger than you, can I?

> *A bitter stare between both women.*

HELEN: *(Cont'd.)* I'm sorry. That was tactless.

> *JOY enters with tea things and a small quantity of sandwiches on a tray.*

JOY: Here we are. How are we all getting on?

> *HELEN dabs her eyes. NORMA pointedly says nothing.*

JOY: Now come on you two! The last post is at five and there are three closing dates this week.

HELEN: No! Two. *The Times*'s cryptic win your weight in tinned squid challenge and the *Telegraph*'s food token puzzle bonanza.

JOY: You're forgetting *The Lady*'s weight watch, shake-mix give away /

NORMA: We said we weren't going to bother with that one. One uses more calories opening the carton than one gains from drinking it. So said Mrs Cooke, the last time I saw her. /

HELEN: That's no use to us. We need to load carbs.

JOY: But Postmaster Hanson said he could sell them on. For cash not stamps.

NORMA: Did he now?

HELEN: *(To JOY.)* It's too dangerous.

NORMA: Shut up, Helen!

JOY and HELEN exchange supportive glances.

NORMA: *(Cont'd.)* If there are Incomers in our town who can afford to eat so much that they need to diet… Well, we will fleece them of every spare penny. It is the moral thing to do. Besides, cash is cash.

HELEN: Mr Brown says if you can't legally work, cash is a trap. He never touches it himself.

NORMA: 'Mr Brown this! Mr Brown that!' Do you ever have any thoughts of your own?

JOY: Norma! Helen was just saying /

NORMA: We're entering all three and that's final.

HELEN: But it's quarter past eleven! We haven't got time.

NORMA: We'll make time… 28 across, 7 letters 'A tune to esteem?'

JOY: Now that's a very hard one isn't it Helen dear? Very hard.

JOY takes a sandwich and then offers one to an eager HELEN.
They are both about to bite down when…

NORMA: There will be no meat sandwiches until we have finished this crossword. Now think!

HELEN and JOY sadly put their sandwiches back down.

NORMA: *(Cont'd.)* Helen? 'A tune to esteem?'… Come on! Your specialism is music. Last letter is T.

HELEN: Is it respect? Yes, I'm certain. It's respect.

NORMA checks, smiles and fills in the blanks.

NORMA: Once again, little Helen earns her keep. Good.

Now Joy? Stop simpering. Get the Sandwich Circle parcels
  packaged up and get them delivered.

JOY: Yes Norma.

> *JOY stands and moves to exit into the Kitchen.*

NORMA: And while you're out, pop into Helen's. She forgot her
  dictionary again.

SCENE 4 – STREET – MID MORNING

MAYA stands with her balloon, face turned up to the sky.

MAYA: Go to the van… A golden rule… But the sun is golden…
  I should go… In a minute…

> *She drops her bag and stretches her arms out.*

MAYA: *(Cont'd.)* A light wind… Thermals found… Variometer
  engaged… And it's safe to launch!

> *MAYA with the balloon, zooms up into the sky.*

MAYA: *(Cont'd.)* 1 thousand… Radiosonde readings begin…
  Bleep. Zuu… Humidity low… Bleep… Up! Detecting fog!..
  Up! Fog cleared! Up! Nimbostratus. 3 thousand, 4 thousand,
  Beep. Wind speed is building… 5 thousand! Stratocumulus! 6
  thousand! Altostratus … UP!.. Uh-oh! Detecting Ice Crystals!
  Goggles on! Cirrocumulus, Cirrostratus… SUN, SUN, SUN!

> *MAYA spins in a joy of movement. But her hand slips and
> the balloon floats out of reach and off.*
>
> *MAYA panics. Then runs after the disappearing balloon.*
>
> *And then the shadows cast by the sun start to stretch…*

SCENE 5 – STREET – MID MORNING

Out of the shadows, JOY appears, slinking along the pavement wearing a head scarf and large dark glasses. She carries a huge, Chamber's Dictionary.

MAYA wanders on, coatless, bedraggled, exhausted. And then she sees JOY and runs towards her, ecstatic.

MAYA: Hello!

> *JOY hesitates, then peers over her dark glasses.*

JOY: Hello?

MAYA: I am Maya. I've been lost for ages! Being lost is not fun.

JOY: You're an Incomer I suppose? Looking for the sea front are you?

MAYA: Am I? I don't know. Are you an Incomer?

> *JOY flashes her tattered green permit at MAYA.*

JOY: No. I am green and local. What about you?

MAYA: I don't have a permit yet. I get one after I merit my birthday test tomorrow.

JOY: Then… You're still a little girl? But what on earth are you doing outside, alone on the street, without your bubble wrap jacket?

MAYA: I wasn't alone. I was with my Daddy. And then he gave me a balloon. Only I lost it. I tried. But I can't find it and now I can't find him.

JOY: Oh you silly billy! That's very… Oh goodness me… You really lost your Daddy?

MAYA: We were having my last day of fun before / everything

JOY: Everything changes for ever. /

MAYA: Yes. But now it's gone all wrong. I've lost my balloon and I haven't had any fun yet.

JOY: You mustn't get yourself upset. That's the last thing your Daddy would want.

MAYA: I'm not allowed to get sad. He only lets me have fun, it's a golden rule.

JOY: He sounds like a lovely Dad. Like a lion is he? Ever so prime?

MAYA: Oh yes. He's the best. We make happy memories every day. He's very strict about it.

JOY: My Daddy was a master of memory making. That's what kept me wiping his nethers right through his final years. I didn't get his brains though. So I don't have a plan.

MAYA: Funny.

JOY: Not for me it isn't.

MAYA: Really it is! Your face. It's so funny! When you talk, little creases ping and pop.

JOY: I can't afford to have it lifted just yet.

MAYA: Lifted?

      MAYA instinctively touches JOY's face.

JOY: Don't!

      JOY snaps her glasses back up and looks around her.

MAYA: Is it far to your house?

JOY: Child? No! You can't come home with me.

MAYA: Why? Grown Ups are supposed to help. You have to help me find my Daddy.

JOY: Maya. You're such a lovely little thing. So keep running. You have your whole life ahead. This street isn't a safe place for an abandoned child. Go to the post office in town and ask for Postmaster Hanson. Tell him Joy sent you. He'll help. He's kind.

MAYA: I'm not abandoned. I told you I'm lost.

JOY: I know. But others might not see that. They might see a windfall… Try and understand.

MAYA: Why don't you want to help me? Are you a bad person?

JOY: No! What a thing to say.

MAYA: I've never met a bad person before.

>*JOY terrified of attracting attention, starts to move away.*

JOY: I am not a bad person. I'm not! I try ever so hard to be good.

MAYA: I'll tell on you… I can remember… Your name is Joy. You have a head scarf. You smell of clean soap! You smile but you are not kind! You hate children and you live on this street.

JOY: I do not!

MAYA: Then why do you have slippers on?

>*JOY looks down… She does indeed still have her slippers on.*

JOY: Alright! Maya? Stop. I'm sorry. Alright. Don't get upset. You can come with me.

>*MAYA instantly lunges and hugs JOY.*

MAYA: Thank you. I knew you were good really. I knew. But Joy, you are so brilliant at pretend! I almost believed you were bad. That was totally fun. I like you.

>*JOY takes MAYA's hand then leads her off to exit.*

SCENE 6 – LIVING ROOM – MID MORNING

HELEN and NORMA are mid-tiff…

NORMA: And I'm telling you. The answer is 'Walkabout'.

>*JOY and MAYA enter. JOY takes off her headscarf and dark glasses as MAYA, shocked, stares at NORMA and HELEN.*

>*HELEN looks up, sees MAYA and freezes.*

HELEN: You're probably right… Put Walkabout, dear. Put whatever you like. That's fine /

NORMA: Thank you. /

HELEN: Because look. Here's Joy returned with / a

NORMA, filling in the crossword doesn't look up, she just thrusts her hand out.

NORMA: *(To JOY.)* Finally. Dictionary. Here please. Was everyone in the Sandwich Circle still with us Joy?

JOY: Yes Norma. But look… Joy found a guest.

Now NORMA looks up and her face goes like thunder.

NORMA: You brought an Incomer into my little house!

JOY: No. She's a little girl. She lost her bubble wrap jacket… She's lost Norma.

HELEN: A little girl? My goodness! It's so hard to tell sometimes. And she's lost? That's awful.

JOY: She asked me to help her. I said that I would try. Maya? This is Norma and Helen.

MAYA's jaw has dropped, looking from woman to woman.

HELEN: Joy? Dear? I'm sorry that the child is lost, but was it really wise to bring / her?

NORMA: Nonsense Helen. Joy? Is she an innocent child who is lost?

JOY: Yes.

NORMA: Then there is nothing to fear. We shall help. That's what decent folk do. Maya come here.

JOY gently pushes MAYA forward.

MAYA: *(To NORMA and HELEN.)* Your creases are even bigger than Joy's! Are you witches? My teacher said all the modern witches had been cooked in an oven. How did you escape the oven?

HELEN: For God's sake! What on earth are they teaching children in school these days? /

NORMA: Now Helen, don't try and deny it. Yes Maya we did escape. We are witches /

HELEN: Oh Norma! Don't /

MAYA: I thought so. Because your skin is so falling off of your face and hands.

NORMA: But we're good witches. White witches. So, don't be scared.

HELEN: Norma? If you don't mind, I would like a quick, private word with you please? /

NORMA: *(To MAYA.)* We witches have wrinkled skin because we're hundreds of years old. But if that frightens you, we can always put our 'face supports' on. Would you like us to do that child?

MAYA: Yes. I think so. You look all wrong /

NORMA: Joy. Bring us our face supports… Go on. Kitchen. Second drawer down.

> *JOY very confused, scurries off.*

MAYA: What is it like? Being an old, old witch with a horrible face and hands?

NORMA: It's jolly good fun. Wouldn't you agree Helen… Helen?

HELEN: It's marvellous.

> *JOY re-enters carrying some very large rubber bands.*

JOY: You didn't mean these?

NORMA: Yes, yes, of course! The face supports.

> *A bewildered look passes between JOY and HELEN as NORMA pulls the elastic band around her jaw and forehead, affecting a kind of instant, if horrific face-lift.*
>
> *She is in some pain. She smiles through regardless.*

NORMA: *(Cont'd.)* Come on Helen. You too. We don't want to give the child nightmares!

> *HELEN reluctantly pulls her band on too.*

NORMA: Maya, my dear child. Do we look better now? Good. So then, how can we help you?

MAYA: I need you to find my Daddy. And I need to have a lot of fun. I need both. Now.

NORMA: I see… That's quite a challenge.

MAYA: But you will help because you are good witches.
So, could you make me a magic potion?

NORMA: Yes.

MAYA: A potion I can drink, which will magic Daddy here?

NORMA: That sounds like a wonderful plan.

MAYA: This is going to be brilliant!

HELEN: Norma, if the child is lost then her Daddy will be worried and /

MAYA: Can I help you make the potion Norma?

HELEN: Norma, this is /

NORMA: Most unusual… Helen is right. We don't usually let little girls help us. But… Alright. Because you are so keen. Yes. You run along outside with Helen here /

HELEN: Norma! /

NORMA: And bring back three special magic things to put in the cauldron.

MAYA: Three magic things! What kind of magic things?

NORMA: Helen will tell you what to look for when you get outside.

> *MAYA leaps up excited and grabs HELEN's hand.*

MAYA: This is totally brilliant fun. Come on!

> *HELEN glares at NORMA. She doesn't move.*

NORMA: Well, off you go Helen. /

HELEN: Have you forgotten? We have three crosswords to finish before 5 p.m. /

NORMA: I haven't forgotten anything. I thought you of all people would relish the chance to prove that you can look after little girls and keep them safe. Don't you want to help the child?

> *JOY is shocked by NORMA's outburst, HELEN is stung.*

HELEN: Of course I'd like to… Of course. Alright… Maya? Come on. Lets go to the garden.

> *HELEN and MAYA exit through the Hall door.*
>
> *NORMA triumphant, pulls the band from her face.*

JOY: Oh Norma. That wasn't kind. Poor Helen. When you know the mix up wasn't her fault.

NORMA: Helen Helen Helen Helen… Do shut up! I want to talk about the child. Joy, she's perfect.

JOY: I thought you would be pleased. Only. I don't really think she's a windfall… She turns 18 tomorrow you see and /

NORMA: Oh… Well, I agree it's a little late to abort so close to the start of the 76th trimester… But on the other hand, she is still legally a child. If we act quickly there will be no / harm done.

JOY: Harm done. Only. No. She told me she has lost her Daddy. So was not abandoned.

NORMA: Stop splitting hairs!

JOY: But what about Helen? Don't you think it would be safer for me to take her to Postmaster Hanson? The lost children posters always go up at the post office so he'd know /

NORMA: We will not waste a windfall! I'll deal with Helen. You go and prepare. We don't want a repeat of the performance you had with the blunt knife and the jittery boy, do we?

> *JOY, very sad, shakes her head and exits into the Kitchen.*

SCENE 7 – GARDEN – LUNCH TIME

The SOUND of the sea and seagulls calling. Every inch of the garden is covered in limp but growing veg.

HELEN is struggling with the pain of the elastic band.

MAYA is running in excited circles…

MAYA: What are the three magic things Helen? Helen? Come on. What are we looking for?

HELEN: I have absolutely no idea. Just pick what you like.

MAYA: That won't work! We have to find three magic things for the potion to find my Daddy and /

HELEN: I don't know. I don't know anything. They send me out so they can have their secret chats all the time. It's demeaning... But we can't always choose our friends, can we?

MAYA: I do.

HELEN: Well then you're very, very lucky aren't you?

MAYA: Why won't you help? I'm meant to be having fun. If you spoil things then I won't have fun things to talk about tomorrow, and Dr Hardy says I have to have fun things to talk about if I want to merit, and you should be good at helping because you're a fucking white witch.

HELEN: Maya! What did you just say?

MAYA: A tomorrow secret slipped out of my bad-things memory box. Everything is going wrong!

> *MAYA curls into a ball and buries her head.*

> *HELEN can take no more. She rips off her elastic band.*

HELEN: Maya. Calm down. Maya? Listen to me. Listen... It's not you! It's this bloody thing. I'm sorry. It hurts. We are not witches. Witches do not exist! We are just desperate old women who can't afford face-lifts. Come on... Calm down now. It's alright.

> *MAYA looks up at HELEN.*

MAYA: You are not witches? You are old women?

HELEN: That's right. Just silly old women trying to get by.

MAYA: Daddy says old people are bad people.

HELEN: If your Daddy met me, do you really think he'd think I was bad?

MAYA: Hmm... No. But he'd be cross with you for giving away a big tomorrow secret?

HELEN: Did I?

MAYA: You told me witches don't exist!

HELEN: Oh God. Well look... I'm sorry. That was silly, but it was a mistake. It's such a long time since I was... If I forgive you for the F word will you forgive me for my little mistake?

MAYA: Four Give?

HELEN: Yes... Forgive? Don't they teach you what forgive means any more? My God. Well. Forgive is a word that gives people permission to rub out a mistake and start again.

MAYA: But Dr Hardy says mistakes are only mistakes if you get caught. He says never get caught.

HELEN: Dr Hardy sounds terribly modern. I'm sure he's right. You listen to him.

> *MAYA stands up. Wipes her eyes. Pinches her face. Smiles.*

MAYA: If you are not witches how will Norma and Joy find Daddy? Cos they have to find him.

HELEN: I don't know. But I do know that they are very resourceful and they always seem to find a way to get what they want. And Norma sounded like she wanted to help you didn't she?

MAYA: Uh-huh

HELEN: So if I know Norma, she'll be planning something special for you right now.

MAYA: Like a surprise?

HELEN: Yes.

MAYA: Is that why they sent us outside?

HELEN: I should think so.

> *MAYA nods, understanding... Kicks her heels.*

MAYA: I don't care what Daddy says about pre-fun. Waiting for fun is not fun.

HELEN: No. Waiting is not fun. It's never fun. I agree.
Your Daddy is wrong about that.

MAYA lunges and hugs HELEN.

MAYA: I don't think Daddy would like you but I do…
You remind me of Ling May. Ling May played games when
we were bored. Shall you and me play a game now?

HELEN: I don't see why not. Games can be / fun.

MAYA: I want to talk about Ling May. I never get to talk about
her. I think you wouldn't mind.

HELEN: Well. I don't see why we shouldn't. Chatting can be fun
can't it. Who was Ling May?

MAYA: She was my Daddy's best Comfort Girl ever! She was
fun. She made cakes. She explained Higgs Boson, clouds,
Schrödinger's cat. She didn't pretend the weather wasn't
there… And she said I was totally Comfort Girl material
because daddies don't care what a Comfort Girl thinks about
as long as they are pretty. She said I was perfect. Then she
disappeared.

HELEN: Oh. Well. I'm not sure Ling May should have said those
things and, actually… I'm not sure if we should really talk
about Ling May if your Daddy doesn't let you.

MAYA: Why doesn't he let me though? He liked her tons and
then he just stopped. Why?

HELEN: I don't know Maya. But… Just try and enjoy this time
instead of worrying. I know things are confusing but it's so
precious. Life will never feel this beautiful again. Never.

MAYA: Why did your eyes just go sad?

HELEN: Did they?

MAYA: Yes.

HELEN: I don't know. Maybe I feel a little bit sad, but /

MAYA: No. You look totally sad. Like when Ling May got sick in
the mornings. Why?

HELEN: You just remind me of someone Maya. I haven't seen her for such a long time / and

MAYA: Why? Is she asleep like Sleeping Beauty?

HELEN: No.

MAYA: Oh dear. She is sleeping but has no Prince to wake her?

HELEN: Do you mean dead?

MAYA: Dead? What is dead?

HELEN: It doesn't matter. Never mind /

MAYA: Is there no Sleeping Beauty and Snow White too?

HELEN: I didn't say that.

MAYA: Hansel and Gretel? Rumpelstiltskin? Are all of them lies?

HELEN: I did not say that. Things are more complicated… Just. You're a clever girl. Try to go with today, but be prepared for a good few shocks tomorrow. That's the way to merit.

MAYA: Good. I want shocks. I've heard they are fun and a lot of blood rushes to your head and you feel light like a cloud. Like you could fly. Go anywhere you want. Go!

MAYA suddenly flies up into the air.

MAYA: *(Cont'd.)* It's stupid that we can't say weather words. I'd love to be a cloud. Wouldn't you?

HELEN: Oh yes, I would. It would be fascinating.

MAYA: I would float until I found adventure. I would be friends with the Sun. I would see everything and know everything. Would you? Would you too?

HELEN: No. I would make a storm cloud and I would rain until the whole world was clean again.

MAYA: You'd be as angry as a cumulonimbus cloud? Really? That's totally cross!

HELEN is somewhat taken aback.

MAYA: *(Cont'd.)* Cumulonimbus make hurricanes.
I love hurricanes. They spin / and

HELEN: Smash. Yes! I would love to be a cumulonimbus cloud.

MAYA: Altocumulus are best. Light like cream cakes.
They go where they want, when they want.

HELEN looks at MAYA and smiles.

HELEN: So very like someone.

MAYA: Your Sleeping Beauty? Is she nice?

HELEN: Natalie? Yes. She was very, very nice. 16. Like you.
Interested in everything /

MAYA: And pretty and clever and well adjusted and full of super-
fun memories.

HELEN: Oh she was.

MAYA: But then she made you sad, so you burnt her?

HELEN: What?

MAYA: Daddy loved Mummy and Ling May but he had to burn
them when they made him sad.

HELEN: No! Natalie was visiting. She was my granddaughter…
I asked her to pop to Norma's. There was a mix up. Norma
asked her to pop to the postbox with a crossword entry.
But when she came back something had happened… She
wouldn't stop crying. It was terrible. Joy and Norma tried to
help me talk to her, but Natalie was… My daughter said it
was unforgivable. I was unforgivable. She /

MAYA: Did you ruin Natalie?

HELEN: No. My daughter said it was still worth trying to mend
Natalie because she was only 16. She got the best therapist.
But she couldn't afford my sentimental attachment fees on top
of Natalie's therapy sessions, so she cut contact with me.
I never hear from them now.

MAYA: Two weeks after Ling May disappeared she sent me a letter that said 'Stop worrying. I met someone new. It's totally fun. Forget about me'.

HELEN: Well, at least she wrote. I would give anything for a letter from Natalie. /

MAYA: It was in Daddy's handwriting. Just like the letters from Mummy.

HELEN: Oh. I see… Well /

MAYA: I know. 'Never mind! Stop it and think about nice things.' That's what Dr Hardy says.

HELEN: I don't think that's such bad advice. Nice things help.

MAYA: But Ling May said everything can not be solved by 'doing more and thinking less'. Who is right Helen? Daddy is perfect and I love him so much but Ling May makes most sense.

HELEN: You really loved her didn't you.

MAYA: She did the best safe touch time, ever. Even better than Daddy.

> *MAYA grabs at unprepared HELEN squeezing into her. They hold each other. And then… Suddenly the pink balloon appears. It floats and stops.*

MAYA: *(Cont'd.)* Look… Helen! Look… It's my fucking balloon!

HELEN: Really dear. If you want to merit tomorrow, you must stop saying that word.

> *But MAYA isn't listening. She flies up and starts chasing the balloon. The balloon starts to eddy away.*

HELEN: *(Cont'd.)* Wait! Wait for me!

> *HELEN lifts off and joins MAYA. They both zoom chasing the balloon. HELEN lunges, catches it, but gravity retakes her and she crashes to the ground… MAYA lands, she watches confused as HELEN groans, holding her ankle.*

MAYA: Aren't you getting up? You look funny… Your face has gone all wrong.

HELEN: Maya. I can't… Just go and get Joy. Tell her I need her.

> *MAYA tries to pull HELEN up.*

HELEN: *(Screaming.)* For God's sake! NO!

> *MAYA stops pulling.*

MAYA: I was helping.

HELEN: I know. It's alright. No it is… Just please. Go and get Joy. She knows how to lift.

> *MAYA nods, takes the balloon from HELEN, exits into the bungalow… Then returns.*

MAYA: You can keep the balloon if it will help you not hurt?

HELEN: It's really fine. Just go and get Joy. Hurry.

> *MAYA exits. As soon as she is gone the SOUND of a gate being RATTLED is heard.*

NOAH: *(Off.)* Hello?

> *HELEN freezes.*

SCENE 8 – LIVING ROOM – LUNCH TIME

Sheets of polythene now cover the floor. In the middle of this is a stool and a bucket.

NORMA sits in the recliner, drumming her fingers.

JOY sits on the other stool sharpening a butchers' knife.

NORMA: Surely the knife must be sharp enough by now? Call the girl in.

JOY: What are you going to tell Helen?

NORMA: I'll just tell her that we sent Maya to the post box.

JOY: Oh no Norma. I don't think we can use that excuse again.

NORMA: Call the girl in.

> *MAYA rushes in through the Hall entrance with her balloon.*

MAYA: Come quick.

JOY hides the knife behind her back.

NORMA: What's wrong dear?

MAYA: Helen was playing and now she has fallen.

NORMA: For God's sake! The woman's an idiot.

MAYA: She's hurting because of it. She can't get up.

JOY: Oh poor thing.

MAYA: Joy will you come and help? We will lift her.

NORMA: No Maya. We will get to Helen in a moment… First we need to finish off your potion.

MAYA: But. Helen is hurting!

NORMA: Do you see where we've put some plastic and our cauldron down?

MAYA: It looks like a bucket.

NORMA: It may do but its not. It's a witches' cauldron. So stop being rude, sit down, close your eyes, say 'magical-smagical-cala-ma-roo' and drop your magic objects in it, now please.

> *MAYA sulkily sits on the stool and JOY moves behind her with the knife…*

NORMA: *(Cont'd.)* Come on Maya. Close your eyes and think of magic and fun.

> *MAYA closes her eyes. NORMA nods. JOY lifts the knife.*

MAYA: OK. But I'm only playing. Helen told me your secret. I know all about you.

> *On hearing this JOY, nervous, drops the knife.*

JOY: What secret? What did Helen tell you?

> *MAYA looks up at JOY then down at the knife.*

MAYA: You dropped that. It's a knife. Knives are really dangerous and sharp.

NORMA: Maya? What secrets has Helen been sharing with you, dear?

MAYA: I'm not allowed near sharp things. Daddy says it is a golden rule.

> *MAYA points at the knife.*

MAYA: *(Cont'd.)* You should pick it up Joy. I could trip and fall on it. It's a golden, golden rule.

NORMA: Joy, pick up the knife.

JOY: I can't. Not now.

NORMA: Pick up the knife.

MAYA: Yes, please pick up the knife, Joy.

> *JOY picks the knife up again, tries to recompose herself.*

NORMA: Thank you Joy. Now, Maya. Please explain what Helen has been saying.

MAYA: That there are no witches! Snow White! or Hansel and Gretel! I know its not real! Pretend is fun but we should go help her up. Then you can tell me your real plan to find my Daddy.

> *JOY looks at NORMA unnerved. NORMA doesn't drop a beat.*

NORMA: Well done Maya. You discovered the first clue. Of course witches don't exist. So now just sit still and we'll tell you about the next part of your adventure.

MAYA: Adventure? What adventure?

NORMA: The adventure that will lead you back to your Daddy, silly.

MAYA: Wow! That's like? That's like? Am I on an adventure? This is totally… But… No. Hang on… We should help lift Helen up first? Because she's hurting. Then we'll start. OK?

JOY: Norma? Would it be better if I did pop and help Helen? /

NORMA: Joy. Helen is pretending. She didn't really hurt herself. It's part of Maya's adventure, remember… So, Maya, please close your eyes. Good girl. Now Joy? Get on.

> *JOY uncertain and shaky raises her knife again.*

MAYA: Are you going to send me to the post box like Natalie? Did you send her on an adventure too? Did she get things wrong? Is that why she got ruined and broke Helen's heart?

JOY screams and drops the knife. MAYA opens her eyes.

MAYA: You dropped the knife again. Pick it up!

JOY: I can't, I just can't. Norma… Helen must know! She knows about the mix up!

NORMA struggles from the chair and picks the knife up.

NORMA: Happy now? Well? What do you say, child?

MAYA: Thank you Norma.

JOY: Poor Helen. Poor Natalie. What an awful, awful mix up.

NORMA: Maya? I don't think Joy is going to help, so I'm going to have to do it instead.

NORMA strokes MAYA's hair. Seeing this JOY lunges and grabs at the knife and they both start to struggle.

JOY: You can't. You don't know what you're doing. You might hurt her.

NORMA: Then you do it then. Like you used to. You used to have it over in a flash.

JOY manages to get the knife from NORMA, but now NORMA grabs for JOY's key fob and rips it from her belt.

NORMA dangles the keys and puts her hand out for the knife.

JOY: Maya, listen to me.

NORMA: Shut up Joy! Or you'll be out.

JOY: Hypothetically?

NORMA: For good.

JOY: Maya? Run!

NORMA: Sit down.

MAYA: I'm confused.

JOY: Just run! Norma is going to /

NORMA: If you say one more word, I'll tell your precious Helen everything. Everything! And that would make what happened to Natalie look like a walk in the park, wouldn't it?

JOY: You wouldn't.

NORMA: I would.

> *MAYA can take no more. She climbs up on top of the recliner and starts to jump up and down.*

MAYA: Stop it! Stop it! STOP IT!

> *NORMA and JOY frantic, rush towards her.*

JOY: Child, don't! Get down!

NORMA: Watch the springs! Get down now!

> *MAYA gets down from the chair. NORMA and JOY rush toward the chair to check it over. NORMA sits and tries the handle. It doesn't work.*

NORMA: *(Cont'd.)* Your precious child has broken my chair!

JOY: I'm so sorry /

NORMA: You are dead to me Joy.

> *JOY is devastated.*

MAYA: Why you are falling out now? When you should be helping me. I have to find Daddy before he finishes reading his estimates. So stop falling out, make friends and help!

> *On the word 'estimates' JOY and NORMA slowly turn to each other and then back to MAYA.*

JOY: Your Daddy reads estimates?

MAYA: Uh-huh.

NORMA: What kind of estimates dear?

MAYA: Daddy is a Utility Inspector and he's doing all of this estate today.

JOY: Does Daddy work for Inspector Stevens?

MAYA: No. Inspector Stevens was a bad lazy man with a permanent contract. Daddy took his job.

NORMA collapses in her recliner.

MAYA: *(Cont'd.)* Daddy is never lazy and his contract is fairer because it's for zero hours. Daddy says no one should get paid for work they haven't done yet /

NORMA: *(To JOY.)* Oh God. Shut her up.

MAYA: Daddy says he helps useless people not be a burden on good people like him and me.

NORMA: *(To JOY.)* You brought this monster into my little home?

JOY: There has been the most awful, awful mix up. Again.

MAYA: I have a fun appointment with Daddy that starts at two pm. It's twelve fifteen already and it's all going wrong. So are you going to make friends and help me or not?

JOY: I'd like to if Norma will?

NORMA: I'm not making friends with a snake in the grass.

JOY: Oh Norma. I didn't know. I didn't.

MAYA: When we fall out at school our teacher says… Come on! Like this… Joy, say you're sorry.

JOY: I'm sorry Norma.

MAYA: Then Norma, you stop saying horrid things and give Joy the keys back that you stole from her.

NORMA: No.

MAYA: She's sad without them. Give her the keys.

NORMA: Do you know? Do you? Because… Why not! It's all over. The larder grows bare, my chair is destroyed, my home-help's against me and now I must have my estimate read. Here. I don't care. Have my bloody keys.

NORMA puts the keys into the hands of MAYA.

JOY: Norma! The child shouldn't have those. Maya, give those keys to me. Now!

MAYA: *(To NORMA.)* Put the knife on the table.

> *NORMA puts the knife down.*

MAYA: *(Cont'd.)* Good. And… Now you are friends again.

JOY: But Maya, you still have the keys. If we're friends… You should give them back to me.

> *MAYA shakes her head, pockets the keys.*

MAYA: *(Cont'd.)* Not until the adventure leads me back to Daddy. So come on. What happens next?

NORMA: Oh all of you, just piss off. Go on. Because its all over. If Daddy is coming. Its the end.

MAYA: He is? Daddy is coming now? But that is brilliant! Why didn't you say?

JOY: It was going to be a surprise… But now, since you know that your Daddy will be arriving any minute, why not tell us all about him… So we can organise a little party for him?

MAYA: A party! For Daddy! Is that the next part of the adventure?

JOY: Yes. Because if we knew all about Daddy, we could make a plan… Couldn't we Norma?

> *NORMA looks at Joy and a tiny spark of hope returns.*

NORMA: Yes. Well I suppose… That could be an / idea.

JOY: Idea / Oh yes. So. Maya… Tell us every single thing you know about your Daddy.

> *MAYA grins and starts spinning around.*

MAYA: A party for Daddy! I love this idea! I love parties! We need to bake buns!

SCENE 9 – GARDEN – LUNCH TIME

HELEN cowers on the floor.

NOAH: *(Off.)* Hello? Hello!

> *The SOUND of a wooden fence being shaken and hit.*

HELEN: Hello! Stop! Stop it… What do you want?

NOAH: *(Off.)* This is number 60?

HELEN: Yes?

NOAH: *(Off.)* Then I'd like to come in.

HELEN: Go to the front door. That's where a stranger should start.

NOAH: *(Off.)* No can do. The new directive says to start at the back. Keeps everyone on their toes. /

HELEN: Directive?

NOAH: *(Off.)* Come on Mrs Pratt. It's the Utility. Here to check your estimate. Let me in please?

> *HELEN is terrified. She tries to get up but she can't.*

HELEN: I'm not Mrs Pratt.

NOAH: *(Off.)* Not Mrs Norma Pratt? You should be. If this is Number 60? It says here /

HELEN: It's wrong. It's very wrong. I'm Helen… Oh God.

NOAH: *(Off.)* I must ask you to allow me access Mrs Pratt.

> *The SOUND of a sudden crunch of splitting wood. NOAH comes on, holding a broken piece of fence.*

NOAH: *(Cont'd.)* The gate was unlocked.

> *NOAH looks down at terrified HELEN.*

NOAH: *(Cont'd.)* No need to look so worried Norma. I'm just popping in to say hello and to tidy up any outstanding paperwork. Once that's done, I'll be on my way.

HELEN: But I'm not Norma. I'm Helen Canning!

NOAH: I'm sure you are Norma. I'm sure you are Helen in your mind. I'm also very certain, that you have not been 37 years of age for quite some time… So let's push on.

HELEN: She put down she was 37 on her estimate?

NOAH: That's what it says here.

HELEN: She's insane.

NOAH: It looks that way. From where I'm standing.

HELEN: I'm not Norma Pratt. I can prove it. I have an amber permit. At home at number 57 /

NOAH: No. Number 57 is on my safe amber list. There is a legally diminished lady living there.

HELEN: I know. That's because that's me! I am Helen Canning and I'm absolutely fighting fit and /

NOAH: You look like you're lying on the floor, unable to stand up to me.

HELEN: For God's sake!

NOAH: Norma? I've got a hot date with the best girl in the world this afternoon, so let's cut the crap. You're old and fucked and certainly not 37. There's no point retesting you /

HELEN: You can't just do that!

NOAH: If you can't stand up to stop me, I can… OK? I'm formally issuing you with a red permit.

> *NOAH starts tapping his pockets.*

NOAH: *(Cont'd.)* If I could just find my red permit pad… I must have left it at the last house I cleared /

HELEN: That was careless. Can you go ahead without a red permit?

NOAH: It's just a formality really /

HELEN: Not to me. If you're going to execute someone, surely you should get the paperwork right?

NOAH: I'll sort it out later. I promise.

HELEN: No. I want to see my red permit. Otherwise it's going to feel like you're murdering me.

NOAH: Don't start throwing that word around. I do my job well under very difficult circumstances, with zero cooperation from clients and a thoughtless word like that can destroy a career.

HELEN: If you turn up to do a job with a sloppy attitude, what do you expect?

NOAH: Alright. You know what? Fine! Don't go anywhere… I'll be right back.

> *NOAH, furious, exits. As soon as he's gone HELEN roars.*

HELEN: Joy? Joy! JOY!

> *HELEN waits… No JOY… Then she remembers her handbag. Suddenly hopeful she crawls to it. Opens it. Hope fades.*

HELEN: *(Cont'd.)* Stupid, old, forgetful woman.

> *HELEN starts to stifle sobs. MAYA enters from the back door and looks down at HELEN, confused.*

HELEN: *(Cont'd.)* Maya. Thank God. Is Joy coming? Where is she?

MAYA: Are you still playing pretend?

HELEN: What?

MAYA: Norma said Joy wouldn't come to help you because your hurt is pretend.

HELEN: She said what? I am not pretending Maya. I can't get up. I don't believe those two.

MAYA: Me neither. They said they were going to plan a party for my Daddy but then all they've done is sit asking stupid questions like 'does your Daddy take bribes?'. What is a bribe?

HELEN: Maya? Please… A very bad man has been here and he's going to come back soon. And when he does, he's going to put me to sleep forever. And all because of an awful mix up.

MAYA: There's been loads of awful mix ups today. Norma and
Joy keep going on about one too.

HELEN: There's no time to talk… No! Don't get sad. Listen.
I know we've only just met but it feels… it feels like we're
friends now. Are we friends Maya?

MAYA: Yes.

HELEN: Well then, this is going to be a lot of fun… Because…
I need you to go to my house. It's just up the road. Number
57. Got that? Good girl. Go into my kitchen, search the
drawers. You'll find a pack of white powder and my amber
permit. Bring them both back here.

MAYA: Is the white powder icing sugar? Are we going to do
baking? Ling May and me used to do baking /

HELEN: I won't lie to you Maya. We're not going to do any
baking. The powder is amphetamine and I'm going to snort
it. I think it might just give me the kick I need to get off the
ground.

MAYA: What is an-feti-meen?

HELEN: I'll explain everything when you get back. But go now.
Don't stop for anything. RUN!

> *MAYA becomes giddy, she goes to the Garden gate, she steps*
> *out and then she stops and steps back inside.*

MAYA: But I'm only a little girl…

HELEN: Maya. I need you to go /

MAYA: I shouldn't be out on the street on my own. It's a golden
rule.

HELEN: It's just across the road /

> *MAYA steps back toward the Garden gate, but stops again.*

MAYA: What if something bad happens like what happened to
Natalie?

HELEN: For God's sake! It won't.

MAYA: But it might?

MAYA comes back into the Garden.

HELEN: A bad man is coming for me Maya? Not everything is about you!

MAYA: My daddy says it is.

HELEN: I thought we were friends. /

MAYA: We are. /

HELEN: It's fun to help friends. /

MAYA: I want to / but

HELEN: You could be helping. You could. You could be helping and… Running like the wind, right now… It's the best fun ever… But now you'll never know.

MAYA looks at HELEN.

MAYA: Running like the wind?

HELEN: Yes, dear. Free, with no one to stop you. Imagine that…

MAYA moves back to the edge of the Garden. Looks out. Looks back at HELEN.

HELEN: *(Cont'd.)* I wonder what Ling May would do?

MAYA suddenly hands HELEN her balloon, then starts to charge around the Garden, revving herself up.

MAYA: She would help! She would be the wind. She would… I will. Watch me! Helen? HELEN! Watch! I'm going. I will… I will…

Until, courage soaring, MAYA finally charges off stage.

MAYA: *(Cont'd.) (Shouting / Going off.)* RUN LIKE THE WIND!

END OF ACT 1

ACT TWO

NORMA slumps down-hearted in her recliner.

JOY: We need a plan. Oh we do. We need one now. Norma? Have you thought of anything yet because it's twelve thirty already and Daddy could be here any second. Any second now.

NORMA: But the child says he's honest and keen and I can't see how we'll / bribe him.

JOY: Bribe him. But there is always a plan. Where has my Norma gone? We just need a plan

NORMA: A plan she says… Will you tell me the truth?

JOY: You can trust me.

NORMA: You lie about sitting in my chair.

JOY: But never about anything else, you have my word.

NORMA: Could I pass for 37? Joy? Tell me… The truth please.

JOY: No.

> *NORMA pulls the elastic back up onto her face.*

NORMA: Now?

JOY: No. Of course not. You're 77. How could you?

NORMA: There. I told you. I knew it. I'm finished.

JOY: But you could pass for late fifties. With a bit of make-up and that band nice and tight /

NORMA: Only, I put down 37 on the estimate…

JOY: You didn't? Oh my God you did. You did! Oh why?

NORMA: You were out collecting treasure and Mr Brown came round. You remember when he bypassed the water meter for

59

us, in return for a leg of ham? I was feeling optimistic.
I thought, I feel 37, so I'll put down 37. Why not? Inspector
Stevens will see me right and /

JOY: 59 maybe. At a push, but never 37. Never, ever, 37. /

NORMA: But 59 is too close to 60. Its all down hill from there. /

JOY: That's not nice. 59 is not 60. It's not… 59 is 59.

NORMA: I do not want her Daddy to come here.

JOY gently puts her hand over NORMA's.

JOY: I know love. But Norma? I think we must now prepare for
the worst. Because Maya's Daddy's is coming. And when he
sees you, I do think he will realise you're not really 37.

NORMA: If he makes me do a reading I won't pass. I wont.

JOY: No. You will if… if… Wait! I've got two paracetamol
saved for a moment like this. If we can just get you some
amphetamine to go with them, nothing will stop you.

NORMA: No one has seen any Billy for months.

JOY: Wrong. I happen to know that Helen has some very nice
speed in her kitchen drawer.

NORMA: Helen?

JOY: She's connected now. Mr Brown is very good to her.
He sorts her out.

NORMA: Helen is really in with Mr Brown? I thought it was just
wishful thinking.

JOY: She's a good deal more than simply 'in' with him.

NORMA: No!

JOY: That's the word on the Vine.

NORMA: That's why she always looks so bloody perky and smug.

JOY: She's a nice person Norma. She's kind. Mr Brown says she
brings out the good in him.

NORMA: How can it be right. She has some fancy man and I lose Graham? I miss him. Every day. Silly, brave, bloody fool. Going out to see if he could help. I said 'sandbags aren't going to help now Graham'… Would he listen?

JOY: But your friends love you Norma. So don't you go giving up on me now. I'm going to get you that speed and if we can get that up your nose, you'll fly through the tests.

NORMA: Do you really think so?

JOY: I know so. So sit up and start doing your face. I'll be back in a tick. You're going to be alright.

> *JOY scurries into the Kitchen and is gone.*

SCENE 2 – GARDEN – LUNCH TIME

HELEN is still on the ground, groaning, holding onto MAYA's balloon. The SOUND of footsteps.

HELEN: Maya. That was quick.

> *But MAYA does not appear. NOAH does. Out of breath. Waving his red permit pad about, triumphant.*

NOAH: Happy now?

HELEN: Please listen. You've made a mistake… A friend of mine has just gone to collect my amber permit. If you'll just wait one moment, please? I can prove I'm not Norma.

> *NOAH starts scribbling onto his red permit pad.*

NOAH: Sadly, once a red permit starts being filled in, the process can't be stopped.

> *NOAH finishes writing, gives HELEN the paperwork then starts filling a syringe as he continues with his patter.*

NOAH: *(Cont'd.)* Your clearance package today will be the standard deal. Unless you'd like to upgrade? For £10 extra you can receive some religious words and a shot of pain relief before I inject the air. Could I interest you in some religious solace and pain relief today?

HELEN: What do you mean by 'religious solace'?

NOAH: I usually stick to C of E.

HELEN: But you have other options?

NOAH: Well yes… But. You want the list don't you? Fine. We can accommodate Roman Catholic, Anglican, Greek Orthodox, Russian Orthodox, Coptic, Anabaptist, Adventist, Methodist, Lutheran and Congregationalist Christians. Or for those of a Buddhist persuasion we do Mahayana, Theravada or Vajrayana endings… If you're a Jainist I can do you too. For any Muslims I do Sunni, Shia, Sufi, Ahmadiyya and Kharijiyyah texts. I can also cater for Narnkaris, Nam-Dharis, Akhand Kirtani Jatha and 3HO Sikhs. Plus Orthodox Jews, Reform Jews, Conservative Jews, and your Hasidic and Kabbala Jews. If you're a Hindu today, no problem. We do Saivites, Shaktas, Vaishnavites and Smartas. The Utility caters for every kind of Useless Individual in a respectful faith focused way… So. Would you like to upgrade today?

> *HELEN looks toward the drive, hoping.*

HELEN: Can I think about it?

NOAH: You think you're funny? I've heard that a million times before.

HELEN: I wasn't being funny. I gave up believing in God when the sea arrived. And I don't have a spare £10. But I do really, really have an amber permit. Please. Please wait.

NOAH: Right. No. Sorry.

> *NOAH kneels down. He takes the syringe, slaps HELEN's arm hard. HELEN's bravado evaporates and her terror returns. She instinctively pulls MAYA's balloon toward herself.*

HELEN: No please. Please don't hurt me.

> *NOAH grabs at the balloon to get it out of the way. And then he stops. And really looks at it. And then at HELEN.*

NOAH: Where did you get this?

HELEN: I don't want to die.

NOAH: I bought a balloon identical to this for my daughter this morning. Exactly like this.

> *HELEN looks at NOAH and suddenly the penny drops.*

HELEN: But. You should wait. You should… Because I think… No I do. I have some information that you might be very interested in. About your daughter. You have to listen /

NOAH: What are you talking about? My daughter is sitting in my van /

HELEN: Only she's not. She didn't do as she was told. Her name is Maya. She's a delightful little girl and it's going to be her 18th birthday tomorrow.

> *NOAH leaps up, suddenly terrified.*

NOAH: Maya!

HELEN: It's no good shouting. /

NOAH: Where is she?

HELEN: Dear? I can help. Calm down and listen. This is the part where you ask what I want /

NOAH: Tell me what you've done with my Maya. It is twelve forty-five. I have a fun appointment with her at Two. She needs a lot of fun right now. Things are difficult.

HELEN: I want to help, but first I'll need certain reassurances… You could start by going and getting me some ice.

NOAH: I don't have ice.

HELEN: I know you have ice and medical equipment in the back of your van.

NOAH: I do not have ice. Christ. This is… I told Maya. I told her to sit in the van. I told her!

HELEN: Well, you're running out of time if you want to bring her back in line.

NOAH: I don't need advice from you on how to bring up my own daughter. /

HELEN: I wasn't giving you advice. I was actually, pretty blatantly threatening you. /

NOAH: I'm the good guy. Me! I'm not the one attempting to blackmail a Utility Inspector.

HELEN: Dear, you're not listening. I'm quite aware of that /

NOAH: Everyone takes the higher ground. I've had it from her Mummy, all the Comfort Girls and now her fucking shrink. When I'm the only one who has always been there.

HELEN: But you weren't there for her, were you? Not this morning. Not when it counted… But you could be again, very soon. If you'd just stop talking and go and get me some ice.

NOAH: Not there for her? Everything is for Maya. I make every fun-memory-session. I have to fuck Comfort Girls, because between work and Maya, when am I supposed to get the time for a meriting social life?

> *NOAH suddenly snaps and starts wildly smashing his chunk of broken fence, on the floor.*

NOAH: *(Cont'd.) (Shouting.)* Not there for her? Not there? Not there! I am there. I am there. I am. Fucking. There.

> *HELEN cowers as NOAH smashes till he is utterly spent.*

NOAH: *(Cont'd.)* Everything is for Maya. But still. She's failing. When all I've ever wanted is for my little girl to merit some happiness.

HELEN: But she's not failing. She's a lovely girl. If a bit sad about you burning Ling May.

NOAH: There you go. Prime example. She won't stop thinking about the wrong things.

HELEN: But that's because she's terribly bright. She just needs stretching /

NOAH: No. She's a daydreamer and questions everything. That needs pushing down /

HELEN: How on earth did intelligence become a bad thing?

NOAH: She doesn't even really like pink. If I can tell, don't you think the test master will notice?

HELEN: She loves this balloon.

NOAH: But she wouldn't have minded it if it were blue. She's just like her Mother.

NOAH starts to well up. HELEN softens.

HELEN: Come on. Chin up. I had a lovely chat with her earlier about life and its pitfalls. She did seem to listen. If you get me some ice, perhaps I could chat with her again?

NOAH: You've been giving my daughter life coach advice?

HELEN: I really didn't mind. She's an absolute delight. And I do remember how hard it is to be a parent. Sometimes an outside eye can be helpful / and

NOAH: What use could an old cunt like you be to my daughter? You know nothing.

Awful, stung silence.

HELEN: Alright. Fine. Well… I'll tell you! Because I still know a thing or two. Yes I do. For instance, I know you have ice for the bodies. And painkillers. I do know that.

NOAH: You've got her inside haven't you?

HELEN: Do I look like an amateur? Look at me… I said look at me! Does it really seem so bloody impossible, that an old person, might be an intelligent human being?

NOAH: I don't know. The sea is at our fucking heels. Who's got time to think now?

HELEN: Well you better start making time. Your prime doesn't last forever. What then?

NOAH: Diminishing doesn't have to be depressing, if you get their memories right at the beginning. Maya will not leave me lying on the floor unable to stand up.

HELEN: A fine plan, only you lost Maya. So if you ever want to see her again, bring me ice and all the antibiotics and painkillers you can lay your hands on. Then we'll talk.

NOAH: I've told you. We don't carry /

HELEN: I happen to know, from a very reliable source that, that, is a lie. Bring me it all.

> *NOAH exits the Garden.*

> *As soon as he's gone, agony sweeps over HELEN again.*

HELEN: *(Cont'd.)* JOY! For God's sake please come now. Joy, Joy, JOY!

> *MAYA enters from the drive, waving the amber permit in one hand and the bag of speed in the other.*

MAYA: Look at me. Look at me. Helen. Look at me! I did it! I did the whole thing on my own. This is the best fun I've ever had.

> *HELEN puts her hand out to MAYA and motions the child to her. MAYA kneels down and HELEN kisses her forehead.*

HELEN: You wonderful, wonderful girl. Now. I need you to be quick. Very quick. Have a look in my handbag. You'll find an old library card.

MAYA: Li-ber-ary? What is Li-ber-ary?

HELEN: Never mind. Just find the card and give it to me.

> *While MAYA starts to go through HELEN's bag, HELEN starts to undo the bag of speed. MAYA hands her the card and HELEN starts to chop out lines.*

HELEN: *(Cont'd.)* You're a very, very good girl. A true friend.

> *HELEN rolls her amber permit and snorts up a line with it as MAYA watches awe struck.*

MAYA: This is brilliant. You really, really, really just sucked that right up your nose!

SCENE 3 – LIVING ROOM – LUNCH TIME

NORMA sits in her recliner staring into a compact, putting on make-up. She smiles a tiny, hopeful, smile at herself.

NORMA: Silly old goose… Carrying on like a frightened girl, wasn't I Graham. When what did you always tell me? 'It's not over till the large lady sings, is it!'

> *But her smile disappears as a SMASHING sound starts to come from the Kitchen (off).*

NORMA: *(Cont'd.)* Hello?

NOAH: *(Off.)* Maya? Maya? Are you there?

NORMA: Oh God… Get out! Get out! You're meant to knock! This is.

> *NOAH appears from the Kitchen entrance. He has part of a split / kicked in front door in his hand.*

NOAH: The door was open.

NORMA: Joy!

> *NOAH lunges and puts his hand over NORMA's mouth.*

NOAH: Where is my daughter?

> *NOAH slowly uncovers NORMA's mouth and looms.*

NORMA: Outside. She's outside.

NOAH: But no. She isn't outside.

NORMA: She isn't?

NOAH: No. I've just come in from outside. So tell me. Now.

NORMA: I don't know. I don't know anything. I thought she was outside.

NOAH: Funny that, because your friend outside? She says she knows.

NORMA: Which friend outside?

NOAH: Mrs Norma Pratt.

NORMA: Norma is outside? But I'm… Really? You're sure it's Norma?

NOAH: Yes. Mrs Norma Pratt is lying outside, attempting to blackmail me into giving her all the drugs we carry in our van, because she says she has my daughter. You, meanwhile, are inside her house saying you don't know her, but you think Maya is outside. I'm confused.

NORMA: She's really trying to blackmail you?

NOAH: Yes.

NORMA: What a dark horse.

NOAH: So you do know her!

NORMA: Are you referring to Mrs Pratt or your daughter now?

NOAH: What?

NORMA: Because I don't know either of them.

NOAH: You said Maya was outside. /

NORMA: No! I was being hypothetical. I suggested looking outside because there are no daughters presently inside. Ergo a lost daughter must be found outside. Logically speaking. Yes?

NOAH: Right you fucking bitch. State your name, address and useful purpose. Now.

NORMA: Look. No. The truth is… I don't know anything about your daughter. I don't even really know Norma. I'm only here because… because… I am an armchair salesperson just trying to sell a chair.

NOAH: Sorry?

NORMA: I didn't say anything before because… Norma disappeared half way through my pitch. I didn't want to jinx things. One doesn't talk about a sale until it's in the bag.

NOAH: But when I arrived you were just sat here, putting make-up on, like you own the place!

NORMA: Yes I was… Because… Surely you know the first rule of sales? It's 'Be Well Presented!' It's terribly important to make a good impression. So I was just touching up.

NOAH looks at her, tries to formulate something to say.

NORMA: *(Cont'd.)* Which explains why I am here and why I'm applying make-up. So now that I've cleared that up for you, I really do hope you feel more assured?

NOAH pauses, thinking, not certain.

NOAH: I'm going to need to see your green permit please?

NORMA: My permit! But no that's not possible. Sadly. No. I'd like to oblige, but I can't. Not just now.

NOAH: Then I'll need to do a reading… I'll need to see your finest star jump please /

NORMA: Wait! No. Because… Look, the truth is this is very delicate. A lady doesn't like to divulge such things. But, if you must know, yesterday, sadly, I turned 59.

NOAH: Is that right?

NORMA: And you of all people should know the law pertaining to 59 year olds?

NOAH: Don't try and teach me my job.

NORMA: I'm just asking. Are you familiar with Article 5 of the General Directive or not?

NOAH: 'If an employee reaches the final year of their useful life, an employer must register their green permit with the Utility, to assure safe transition into their new diminished lifestyle'.

NORMA: So. As my boss is complying with Article 5, I can not avail you with my permit today.

NOAH: I'm going to lay this out. And then we'll see how clever you are. I'm going to find my girl. Then I'm going to enforce Norma's red permit and end her useless life. And, once she's cleared, everything here becomes mine. Everything. Sold, or unsold.

NORMA: But you can't do that! This chair is company property /

NOAH: Article 15, 'All possessions in the residence of a cleared Red Permit holder, automatically, on the occasion of their demise, shall pass to the Utility.' Which I take to mean me. Because I work hard and every Utility Inspector has a side line in antiques now. But… if you stop pissing me off I may be able to be convinced to let you keep your recliner once I've cleared her. If you choose to cooperate. Do you want to cooperate today?

NORMA: It goes without saying, sir, that I am a great supporter of the very important work you do. If there is anything I can do to help. Anything at all, then just say.

NOAH: I'm glad you said that. I think Norma has my daughter in this house. I don't know how many associates she has. It may become dangerous but I'm going to search the property.
I want you to sit here and watch the entrance for me. Can you do that?

NORMA: It would be a privilege. Only I'm sure I would have noticed if there was a little girl locked in the bungalow.
I do wonder if you might be better trying outside again?

NOAH: I am the law enforcement expert here. Are you with me or not?

NORMA: Absolutely. Of course. Of course. I was just trying to help.

NOAH: I'm going in.

> *NOAH enters the Hall door and as he does so the Hall lights up. For the first time, it can be seen. It includes several normal doors but one REINFORCED METAL DOOR.*

NOAH: *(Cont'd.)* Maya. MAYA! Sweetie… If you can hear me, call out for Daddy. Maya!

> *NOAH is smashing at doors, entering them. Looking inside then moving on. Until he gets to the Metal Door. He smashes at it over and over but he can't break it down. The light darkens on the Hall as NOAH keeps smashing at the door.*

NORMA all the while sits in the Living Room, cringing with every CRASH and SMASH she hears.

And then NOAH reenters the Living Room, sweating hard.

NORMA: You didn't find her then? I said I didn't think you would.

NOAH: In all my years in the Utility I've never come across a door like it.

NORMA: I thought you were looking for your daughter?

NOAH: There's something wrong in this house. Something very, very wrong.

NORMA: I know that you said Norma has been blackmailing you, but other than that, I have to say she appears to me to be a very respectable lady. I'm sure this house is just fine /

NOAH: I have to go and get my heavy tools. She's got my Maya behind that metal door. I'm telling you, I've never come across a door I couldn't break down before. If there was nothing to hide in this house, that door would not exist. I need your help… Do you swear that you are a good and useful member of your community?

NORMA: I do.

NOAH: Be my eyes and ears for me while I run to get my tools. Can you do that?

NORMA: Of course. Of course… It is an honour to be asked.

NOAH exits through the Kitchen. As soon as he is gone…

NORMA: *(Cont'd.)* Joy, Joy, JOY! Where is the speed… For God's sake, come on!

SCENE 4 – GARDEN – EARLY AFTERNOON – CONTINUOUS

MAYA: Again! Again! Again!

> *MAYA watches fascinated as HELEN cuts a final line.*

JOY: *(Off, running on.)* Helen! Someone has broken in at 57, messed up your kitchen and stolen all your billy!

> *JOY scurries in from the drive / garden entrance at a pace.*

HELEN: Hang on. Almost there…

> *JOY reaches HELEN, just in time to see…*

JOY: Helen? Oh God. No!

> *… HELEN snorting up the last line and then lying back.*

JOY: *(Cont'd.)* Oh Helen. You took the speed. Why?

HELEN: Because I've been on the ground for some time. And I'm in trouble and frankly it seemed like a good idea. In actual fact? Taking the speed was the only idea I had left.

JOY: Well you're not in as much trouble as Norma is now. I'll need what you've got left over.

HELEN: There isn't any. I snorted it all.

JOY: No! You had a huge bag of billy! How could you have finished it? Norma hates it when the Sandwich Circle don't share. Why would you do this to her?

HELEN: I'm sorry. I haven't done anything to Norma. I didn't know she wanted my… How did you know about my stash? Do you go through my drawers? I thought you were my friend?

JOY: I am. But Norma was counting on getting that speed. How will she ever pass her test now.

> *MAYA's attention is drawn to the plastic bag that the speed came in. Unnoticed by JOY or HELEN, she picks it up.*

HELEN: And what about me! If you had come and helped me sooner I could have told you. A bad man is coming. I have risked everything to protect, Norma. Everything.

JOY: But we already know about the bad man. That's why Norma needs the speed!

MAYA: Joy and Helen? Please don't worry. My Daddy is coming at 2 p.m. for his party remember? If the bad man does anything bad, my Daddy will stop him. That's what my Daddy does.

HELEN: Well that's a relief. But the bad man could turn up before your Daddy arrives couldn't he? Isn't that right Joy?

JOY: Oh yes. Of course. And that's why I must talk to Norma. I'm sorry Helen.

HELEN: Why do you always take her side? I thought you were my friend too!

JOY: Oh I am. I am. I think you're a lovely lady. I do.

HELEN: Then why can't you see how I feel? After everything you and Norma have put me through.

JOY: Put you through? What are you saying? What have we put you through?

HELEN: What do you think? Look at me! I'm lying here on the floor! I'm not an idiot!

>   *JOY, backs away from HELEN and exits through the back door.*

HELEN: *(Cont'd.)* Joy? JOY! For God's sake…

>   *HELEN lies back and roars with frustration.*

MAYA: Are you cross with me?

>   *HELEN slowly leans up.*

HELEN: Maya I'm not cross with you. You are a true friend. I'm just running out of time.

MAYA: I'm sorry that you're sad because this has been my fourth best day ever. It's been totally fun. I've had shocks and lost my balloon and found my balloon and made new friends and learnt tomorrow things and broke into a house and saw you suck speed and I bet Maddy O'Brien isn't having half as much fun on her boring old fun-memory-package is she?

HELEN starts to smile.

HELEN: No. I bet she isn't.

MAYA: You started smiling again. You have a nice smile. So kind.

HELEN: Get ready to see lots of it. I'm coming up… Thank God.

MAYA: You're not. You haven't moved. You're still on the floor.

HELEN: Yes I am. Yes. Yes. YES!

HELEN puts her hand out to MAYA.

HELEN: I think I'm ready. Pull.

MAYA: I don't want to hurt you.

HELEN: You can't hurt me now. I'm… I'm… Come on Maya!
On three…

MAYA: 1… 2… THREE!

HELEN: 1… 2… THREE!

With a huge effort MAYA pulls HELEN up from the floor.

MAYA: We did it!

*MAYA and HELEN hug. But then HELEN looks at her watch
over MAYA's shoulder.*

HELEN: Look at the time. Its ten past one! Your Daddy is going to
be here any minute.

MAYA: Which means the bad man can't get you.

HELEN: That's right. That's right. That's… Oh my lips…
Here we go.

MAYA: Are you hurting Helen?

HELEN starts licking her lips.

HELEN: No. Of course not. It's the speed. It's wonderful.

MAYA: Can't I please have some? I looked in the bag and there's
a tiny bit left, look. And Joy said that taking speed could help
Norma pass a test, so if I took some maybe it would help me
pass my birthday test tomorrow?

MAYA shows HELEN the plastic bag she picked up. HELEN shakes her head. Takes the bag. Dabs up the last bits.

HELEN: Maya. No dear. Listen please. Speed is a… It's a naughty drug. It's very bad for your heart but it makes one feel wonderfully alive. And Mr Brown. God love him, he's always slipping me some. Things feel better and I don't get so hungry and Mr Brown makes me feel so optimistic… So sometimes I succumb. But young people shouldn't. And besides, if they find it in your blood test tomorrow, I promise, you will not merit… But you didn't hear that from me. Now look. I need you to listen. Because! I'm starting to chatter. That's the way the speed, goes with me. At the start. When I'm coming, up. It can be hard to concentrate but it's important that you listen and do what I say. Do you understand?

MAYA: Is Mr Brown your Comfort Boy?

HELEN: Goodness what a thought! Well… Maybe. I'll ask him what he thinks about that later.

MAYA: You love him though?

HELEN: I do! I feel guilty. I do. I don't deserve to be happy. I lost my granddaughter. I broke my daughter's heart and who can blame her for tearing up our sentimental attachment? Really, it's a sign of what a nice person Sonja is that she didn't report me or have me burnt. Just cut off all contact. But honestly in her shoes? I'd have done the same. Because you don't lose your own grandchild do you? You keep her safe. It's the least I should have done… But when Sonja, stopped the food parcels things got very bad, Maya. I was sad… I only had Norma and Joy. So when Mr Brown walked into my life. Well, fell in. He was stealing the lead off my roof, but we don't talk about that any more. It was wonderful. He doesn't laugh at my books and he likes my smile and slowly, even though he's as wide as the ocean's deep, I find I have something to live for. And there lies my problem. No don't speak. You can write down any questions that you have and we'll come back to them later. Alright?

MAYA: I don't have any paper. I lost my rucksack?

HELEN: There's a notebook in my handbag. You've got it? Good because here's my problem. I have something to live for and I don't want to die yet. I'm not ready Maya. I'm not.

MAYA: Die?

MAYA puts her hand up.

HELEN: *(Cont'd.)* No. I told you. If you have a question…
You have one?

MAYA: I have five.

HELEN: Well, write them down.

MAYA starts to scribble furiously.

HELEN: *(Cont'd.)* The thing is, and I don't want to scare you, but I think, after our chat today? I think you're old enough. Goodness I can't get this out quickly enough. Mouth full of ideas. I feel so good. Really good. My leg isn't hurting. Which is good because when your Dad gets here /

MAYA: Joy and Norma are going to throw him a party!

HELEN: Shh! I know. You said. Not another word. Listen. Do you remember how Ling May, what a lovely name that is! We've spoken so much about her today, haven't we? Such a lovely time. I've loved meeting you. But Ling May. Yes! Do you remember how you kept secrets with her? The Tomorrow secrets you kept secret from your Daddy?

MAYA opens her mouth to speak.

HELEN: *(Cont'd.)* Just nod. Do you remember? Just nod.

MAYA nods.

HELEN: *(Cont'd.)* Good girl. Well I thought we could do a similar thing. We could keep a secret from your Daddy and that would give him a surprise. Would you like to give your Daddy a surprise?

MAYA: Yes!

HELEN: I knew you would. Because secrets are fun. You know what else is fun? Playing jokes. I thought we could play a joke on Daddy. Just for fun. To make him smile?

MAYA: Yes. I love playing jokes on Daddy.

HELEN: So I thought you could hide and then pop out and surprise him!

MAYA: I love hide and seek!

HELEN: I knew you would. Natalie loved hide and seek too. I hope you are good at hiding. Are you good at hiding? Just nod dear, I can't stop now.

> *MAYA nods.*

HELEN: *(Cont'd.)* Good girl. So in a moment I'm going to ask you to go and hide in the bungalow. You find a secret place that no one else knows and you don't come out until I call you. Even if your Daddy calls, you keep hiding. You keep hiding until I call for you. Then you come out /

> *MAYA starts to jump around excited. She brings JOY's keys out of a pocket and waggles them around.*

MAYA: Can I use Joy's keys?

HELEN: Joy gave you her keys?

MAYA: Uh-huh. I will so totally find a totally secret place. Can I use them? Can I?

HELEN: Yes, yes of course you can. If Joy gave you her keys, she wouldn't mind you using them would she?

MAYA: This is going to be totally, totally fun. I love you. I told you, you are just like Ling May!

> *And MAYA lunges and hugs HELEN. HELEN peels her from her. She's getting anxious now.*

HELEN: So off you go and hide. Alright? Off you go!

> *MAYA carrying her balloon exits through the back door.*

> *With MAYA gone. HELEN takes a moment. Then pulls her Balaclava from her handbag, puts it on and then with great determination hobbles to exit through the gate.*

SCENE 5 – HALL – EARLY AFTERNOON

MAYA creeps through the Hall corridor with her balloon, looking at the doors.

MAYA: *(Whispering.)* Fffffffff… Stratosphere…

> *She tries a door, looks in, shuts it, creeps on.*

MAYA: *(Cont'd.) (Whispering.)* Mesosphere… Beep…

> *She cracks open the door opening into the Living Room. As she does this the LIVING ROOM lights up. Revealing Norma and Joy mid-conversation.*

MAYA: *(Cont'd.) (Whispering.)* Kármán line… Bleep…Float… Reading…

JOY: *(Off.)* Now Norma don't panic… Remember, you're clever. We'll find a plan C.

NORMA: *(Off.)* I can't believe it. That selfish little slattern really took all of my billy.

> *MAYA carefully closes the door. And the LIVING ROOM light on HELEN and JOY fades.*

MAYA: *(Cont'd.) (Whispering.)* Ice Crystals… Zooo… Not in there…

> *MAYA creeps on until she stands before the big metal door. She tries the door, it's locked. She smiles. She tries a key, no good. She tries another. it opens.*

MAYA: *(Cont'd.) (Whispering.)* Beeeeep…Thermosphere, Ionosphere, Aurora, Aurora, Aurora!

> *She steps inside the door and it sucks shut behind her. A pause and then the distinct SOUND OF MUFFLED SCREAMING starts coming from within. The door handle rattles and rattles. But it will not open.*

SCENE 6 – LIVING ROOM – EARLY AFTERNOON

JOY twitches at NORMA's side. NORMA still sitting in her recliner thumps the arms and roars.

NORMA: It's no good!

JOY: You're sure?

NORMA: Get the suitcase. It's too late. We must leave.

JOY: Leave our little home? No! You're being hasty.

NORMA: With good reason Joy. Have you seen how quickly I can walk these days? Without that billy I will need the longest head start I can get.

JOY: You can't go outside. No! I still think with a little bit of make-up and my Paracetamol we can get you through a reading. You've got a will of steel.

NORMA: Joy, the game is up. It's no good… Daddy has been here and everything is over.

JOY: Daddy has been here in this room! But… When? Did he ask to see your estimate?

NORMA: He did. But I managed to avoid that by convincing him that I was a soft furnishings sales person simply here to sell this recliner to Helen.

JOY: To Helen?

NORMA: Helen told Daddy that her name is Norma and that she has abducted Maya and will only give the child back if Daddy brings her all the contents of his van.

JOY: No! Helen really said that?

NORMA: That's what Daddy told me.

JOY: But Maya's outside.

NORMA: I know. I tried to tell him that /

JOY: I never thought I would say this of Helen, but I'm shocked. I think she knows. She said as much when I was outside. That's why she snorted all the speed. She's taking revenge.

NORMA: I told you. I told you she was a little Incomer bitch, didn't I?

JOY: You did. Oh you did. But I couldn't see it. Even so, I think you were unwise to risk using the soft furnishings salesperson con on Daddy. You know every other Utility Inspector has a little second hand furniture business on the side? He could have wanted to buy your chair and then what would you have done?

NORMA: I would have taken the money and run. Thanks to his little brat the chair is broken, remember.

JOY: Don't think like that. We will get it fixed. We'll make it like new again, dear. You'll see /

NORMA: Don't be ridiculous! Just because you want to make things better doesn't mean they mend. Broken things stay broken. Haven't you learnt anything from what happened to Natalie?

A horrible silence. JOY is very upset.

JOY: We said we'd never discuss it again. When you know… I was just trying to help you.

NORMA: Trying to help! Trying to be nice! You sound like little bloody Helen! Back stabbing bitch! It's because of her that Daddy has discovered the larder!

JOY screams.

JOY: Daddy's been in the larder as well?

NORMA: No, but he's coming back here, any moment to force the larder door open. Do you see now Joy? It's not just me, it's you too. We both have to leave.

JOY: But wherever shall we go?

NORMA: We'll bunk down in Mrs Khan's darkroom and then we'll see how we go.

JOY: You'll never make that walk.

NORMA: I'm going to have to try because if Daddy returns with his special tools, takes the metal door down and sees inside our larder, you and I are finished. So get the case and pack!

> *JOY exits off into the Kitchen.*
>
> *NORMA hastily goes through reference books and papers.*
>
> *JOY returns from the Kitchen with a battered old case and NORMA throws crosswords books and HELEN's* Chamber's Dictionary *into it.*

JOY: Should we really take Helen's dictionary?

NORMA: It's the least that bitch can do for us now /

> *JOY runs off into the Kitchen again.*

NORMA: *(Shouting after her.)* I'll need my cardigan. And… Don't forget the sheet of picture stamps!

> *JOY runs on with a moth-eared cardigan, a tabard, a pair of Wellington boots and a sheet of stamps.*
>
> *JOY throws these into the case.*

NORMA: Hurry up!

> *JOY is about to close the case then stops.*

JOY: Oh Norma. I'd forget my head if it wasn't screwed on.

> *JOY picks up the plate of sandwiches and slams it into the case too, then sits on it and start zipping it up.*

NORMA: Come on Joy. Daddy will be back here any minute!

> *Suddenly, HELEN (still in her balaclava) carrying a huge holdall, appears, hobbling in from the Kitchen.*
>
> *The three women stop and stare at each other.*

JOY / NORMA / HELEN: Going somewhere?!

NORMA: You have a nerve. Coming back into my little home when you've stolen my identity to blackmail a Utility Inspector. Butter wouldn't melt. Ungrateful, little bitch!

JOY: And there was me, believing you were nice. Norma tried to warn me. She said 'Don't trust her' But I let myself love you!

When you're nothing but a selfish Incomer in your horrible jumpers, soft shoes and slacks.

HELEN throws down the holdall and peels off her balaclava.

HELEN: Do you really think I could be capable of stabbing you in the back? I've been trying to protect Norma all along… Have a look! Look at what I've done for the Sandwich Circle.

HELEN stares at NORMA and JOY. JOY begins to squirm. NORMA holds HELEN's gaze, unrepentant.

NORMA: Have you been practicing that little speech? A little speech from little Helen /

HELEN: Don't you dare! Don't you put me down when I look out for you. Because I do. Despite the fact that you are horrible people, still you're the best friends I have left. So I do. I do. And I am a good friend… Don't you dare 'little Helen' me. Don't you dare.

NORMA: If we had more time, we'd love to chat. But sadly, we have to go. Joy bring the case.

NORMA turns her back on HELEN and starts to hobble out of the room and into the Kitchen.

Only JOY does not follow on. Her eye has been caught by the holdall. She unzips it. She starts pulling out bottles of pills. She becomes excited.

JOY: Norma. Wait! There are some arthritis pills here that we haven't been able to get hold of for years.

NORMA turns back. A sheepish look passes between her and JOY.

NORMA: Really… Oh / dear

JOY: Dear. We jumped to conclusions about Helen. There has been another little mix up.

NORMA: This is quite a haul. This is? Helen. This is excellent work.

HELEN nods.

HELEN: I told you.

JOY: Oh Norma. I think we owe Helen an apology. Norma? Don't we?

> *NORMA locks eyes with HELEN. NODS and is about to say something when…*
>
> *There is a HUGE CRASHING SOUND in the Kitchen.*
>
> *All the women turn to find NOAH looming in the Kitchen doorway with a bin liner full of heavy tools.*
>
> *NOAH watches the three women handling his stolen pills.*

NOAH: That's where my holdall went! Those are my pills! How did you break into my van?

HELEN: I told you. I'm connected. So, I know a thing or two.

> *JOY and NORMA glance at each other, quite taken aback.*
>
> *But NOAH doesn't miss a beat, he's too busy dragging his tools through the room, toward the Hall door exit.*

NOAH: You may be connected love. But I know where you have her. That metal door is coming down and if one hair on her head is touched, I will finish you all.

> *NORMA and JOY panic. JOY picks up the suitcase and NORMA stumbles toward the Kitchen. But not HELEN.*

HELEN: Don't you fucking dare underestimate me Daddy.

> *NOAH, NORMA and JOY all stop and turn to look at her.*

HELEN: *(Quiet and calm.)* Be quiet and listen… If you do what I say, now, quickly and calmly, you will see your daughter again. She will be in the very best of health and spirits. If you don't. If you do anything other than what I tell you to do, now or in the days and weeks to come, an associate of mine will kill her, then kill you… We will come for you. Do you understand?

JOY: Oh Helen. What has got into you?

HELEN: *(Quiet and calm.)* Shut up Joy. Daddy? Did you hear what I said?

NOAH, visibly unnerved by this, nods.

HELEN: Good… You're very lucky. I did think about keeping her, because let's face it, you're a disaster as a parent. What do you think you've been doing today? On the child's second most important day of her life? Leaving her alone with a balloon? Anything could have happened to her. It's lucky that we three diminished but still legal ladies were here to help out /

JOY: Two diminished ladies. One of us is still prime. I have a year of green left in me yet! /

HELEN: Joy, I won't ask again. I'm in the middle of a delicate negotiation.

JOY: Sorry /

HELEN: The fact that your daughter was delighted to spend the day with us, suggests to me, that you need to pull your socks up, dear.

NOAH: You have no idea how hard it is! You have no idea /

HELEN: Yes I do. I wonder sometimes how your generation think you all arrived. By Stork?

NOAH: Stork? What? What are you on about?

HELEN: There was a time when there were lots of birds…
We didn't just have seagulls… Oh never mind. The point is, we've given Maya a fun day, she's loved every minute and made wonderful memories. So now, no thanks to you, she has a chance of meriting tomorrow.

NOAH: You can't talk to me like this. Don't make me call for back up!

HELEN: Oh please. Don't insult me. We know they dock your wages if you ask for support.

JOY: It's all over the Vine. Utility Inspectors can't afford to call for back up.

NOAH looks from HELEN to NORMA to JOY

NOAH: She'll come back to me happier than she was before? Guaranteed?

HELEN: Guaranteed.

> *A silence while NOAH weighs up his options.*

NOAH: OK. What do you want?

HELEN: A legal amber permit, made out in the name of Norma Pratt.

> *NORMA and JOY look at each other, surprised but hopeful.*

HELEN: *(Cont'd.)* An arrangement, where you become my eyes and ears in exchange for some perks.

> *NORMA's face falls.*

HELEN: *(Cont'd.)* Working for us is not without its benefits. Joy's talents here are legendary and if you would like to take advantage of her services, then that can be arranged, can't it Joy?

> *JOY looks at NORMA. NORMA upset, nethertheless nods at JOY. JOY snaps on a yellow rubber glove.*

JOY: I could give you a little trial run in the recliner now, if you like Daddy? As long as you're careful where you make your deposit. Because broken or not, this is a very nice chair.

NOAH: I don't want a 'trial run'. I want… I tell you what I want. I want my daughter back!

> *JOY's chin sinks.*

HELEN: And we want the amber permit and an inside eye. Do you understand? Do we have a deal?

NOAH: You guarantee my daughter will come back to me unharmed?

HELEN: She'll come back happier than she was when she left you. What's your decision?

> *NOAH looks at the women. And then he nods.*

NOAH: OK… I'll do it. I'll do the paperwork. You go and get me my Maya.

HELEN smiles a lovely smile.

HELEN: That's a very wise decision. I'll pop and get her now.

NOAH starts scribbling on his amber permit pad, while HELEN exits off into the Kitchen.

HELEN: *(Off stage.)* Maya? Maya darling… You can come out now.

NORMA slumps into her chair, feeling redundant.

JOY: This is lovely news.

HELEN enters from the Kitchen, looking around.

HELEN: Maya dear… Out you come!

JOY: Lets have some tea, to celebrate? And maybe some sandwiches?

JOY exits into the Kitchen.

HELEN: What a nice idea. A round of sandwiches would be lovely.

That's the final straw. NORMA, livid, can take no more.

NORMA: *(Shouting.)* Joy, get back in here! There will be no sandwiches! This is still my home! I call the shots!

NOAH looks at NORMA, confused.

NOAH: I thought you were the soft furnishing sales person? When did you move in?

A look passes between HELEN and NORMA.

HELEN: Did she tell you that? She's always telling visitors that story. She's not… The chair is mine… She's just here because… She's Joy's mother… Isn't that right Joy?

JOY arrives back from the Kitchen with sandwiches.

JOY: Well. Yes.

HELEN: Joy's my live-in help. 'Mother' here likes to come and sit with us, but she does get a little bit confused sometimes. Don't you dear?

NORMA glares at HELEN but says nothing.

NOAH: *(To JOY.)* The Sentimental Attachment fees for that must cripple you. But if you can afford it you can spend your money how you like. It's a free country.

HELEN: Joy is so devoted to the funny old thing, aren't you Joy? Mother's paid for up until June.

NORMA glares at JOY as she stands hugging the sandwiches

NOAH: *(To NORMA.)* Lucky old cow. Living the dream here love, aren't you.

HELEN: Joy can dig out her paperwork, if you need to see it?

NOAH: No. Really… I just… I just want to get my Maya back safe, thanks. If we could get on?

HELEN: Of course… Maya. Little love is playing hide and seek.

HELEN smiles and exits into the Hall.

JOY offers sandwiches to NORMA and NOAH but they both decline. So she starts devouring them herself, avoiding eye contact with NORMA who glares at her all the while.

SCENE 7 – HALL – EARLY AFTERNOON

HELEN searches the Hall.

HELEN: Maya! Out you come now… Maya!

Slowly, the solid steel door starts to rattle while muffled screaming begins to leak from within again.

HELEN, shocked, tries the huge metal door.

HELEN: *(Cont'd.)* Maya?

The door won't open.

MAYA: *(Off.)* Helen. Please! There are sliced legs and half a boy's face! The key snapped! I can't get out /

HELEN: Maya? Oh my God /

MAYA: *(Off.)* Helen! Get me out. Get me out. Get me out!

HELEN: Alright dear… Calm down. It's alright… Remember. We're having fun… Just wait a moment. I'm going to go and get help.

SCENE 8 – LIVING ROOM – EARLY AFTERNOON

HELEN ashen, attempts to breeze back in from the Hall.

NOAH is scribbling at his paperwork.

HELEN: Joy dear, do you have the key for the cupboard in the hallway please?

JOY: The solid steel cupboard door?

HELEN: Yes, there is only one cupboard in the hallway. It seems to be locked and I need to get in.

JOY and NORMA exchange a horrified look.

NORMA: Why would you want to go testing the locks of the doors in someone else's home?

JOY: She means, in your home, but in a home where I carry the keys. So really the responsibility of looking after the locks is mine. I think that's what you meant… Isn't it… Mum?

NORMA: Yes, dear, that's exactly what I meant. Exactly so.

NOAH: Is everything all right?

HELEN: Oh yes, everything's fine. I just need the key. Joy, please?

JOY: But no one ever goes in that cupboard. It is always kept locked.

HELEN: There's just a… a little gift I'd like to get out of it for Maya. Before she goes home.

NOAH: I'm not issuing this permit if there's a problem.

HELEN: There is no problem, is there Joy?

JOY: Problem? No.

NOAH: So, where is she?

NORMA and JOY glare at HELEN.

HELEN: She's just using the lav.

NOAH: Oh right. Well then she'll be hours. Maya takes forever in the toilet.

>*All the women grin at NOAH but as soon as he's gone back to the paperwork they glare at each other.*

NORMA: I can't imagine that there are many things kept in a cupboard that a little girl would want.

HELEN: Joy would I ask unless there was a very, very good reason?

JOY: No.

HELEN: So. The key? Right now please.

JOY: I don't have it.

NORMA: You don't?

JOY: No.

NORMA: Well then who does? Who on earth does! Because if the designated key holder can't keep track of the bloody keys, then what is the world bloody coming too?

JOY: *(To NORMA.)* I don't know… I don't… They were… No it was you! When we were playing the 'witches' game, it was you! You gave Maya my keys.

>*NORMA's face falls.*

HELEN: Well now. Here's a pickle. Joy? If you don't have a spare, perhaps you'd be happy to come and help me break the cupboard door down?

>*NORMA and JOY look at each other in utter terror now.*

JOY: But that's not quite in my job description? It's reinforced steel. I might hurt my back.

NOAH: Ladies? Why don't you let me break the door down? It's what I do. I'm very quick.

NORMA: No!

HELEN: Mother is right. I really couldn't put a guest to that kind of trouble.

NOAH: It's no trouble. And to be honest, any Utility Inspector coming round here would be suspicious to find a door that well reinforced. A door like that looks like you've got something to hide. If I'm working for you now, that's my first bit of advice, right there.

HELEN: Right.

NOAH: The permit's all done.

> *NOAH hands HELEN the filled out amber permit*

NOAH: So. I'll bring the door down. You go and get Maya.

> *All three women look at each other, hoping that one of them will come up with something to stop him. But…*
>
> *NOAH drags his tools and exits out into the Hall.*
>
> *As soon as he's gone HELEN slams the door behind her and puts her back to it.*

HELEN: *(To NORMA and JOY.)* What have you done? Why is Maya locked in that cupboard, screaming?

> *The SOUND of muffled screaming (off) is heard.*

JOY: Oh my God. The child is in the larder? But that's terrible. Norma how could you?

NORMA: I didn't know she was in there. Helen said she was safe.

> *The SOUND of a door being SMASHED down.*

HELEN: Larder? What Larder? What is in that cupboard? She said she could see sliced faces!

> *There is an ALMIGHTY CRASH (off)…*

MAYA: *(Off.)* Witches Daddy! Witches!

HELEN: What in God's name, have you two done?

NOAH: *(Off.)* Oh my God… Oh Christ!

MAYA: *(Off.)* Daddy, Hansel and Gretel are dead! Someone hung them upside down and cut them up.

The door behind HELEN's back starts to shudder (off).

HELEN: I can't hold him off on my own.

JOY and NORMA go to help HELEN block the door.

NORMA: *(To HELEN.)* Where did you think the sandwiches come from? You knew. You chose to look away.

JOY: Stop it Norma. You're wrong. Helen is a nice lady. Unlike… Oh how could you have put Maya in the Larder? When you know what happened to Natalie? It's unforgivable.

NORMA: I did no such thing! Joy, I promise dear, I did not know the child was in the larder.

HELEN: *(To NORMA.)* You put my Natalie in that room? You ruined her! Why? How could you have done that?

More SCREAMING (off). A huge SMASH at the door now, which the three women only just manage to hold back.

And then a sudden calm. HELEN, JOY, NORMA stand shoulder to shoulder, backs against the door.

NORMA: You don't understand. We were trying to do the right thing. We thought Natalie was a windfall. We stopped when we realised she was your grand daughter. We wouldn't ever eat a neighbour's grandchild! We are not / animals!

JOY: Animals. We told her we wouldn't hurt her if she would just go home, forget about the larder and think about nice things. We didn't mean to ruin her. It was just an awful mix up.

NOAH crashes back into the house through the Kitchen, dragging a shell-shocked MAYA behind him.

NOAH grabs HELEN and drags her to the armchair.

HELEN: What are you doing? No. Please Daddy, Norma tell him!

MAYA cowers watching everything with wide eyes.

HELEN: I didn't do anything. I don't know what is in the cupboard.

JOY: I'm so sorry. Maya, you shouldn't have been inside the larder. Just an awful mix up /

NOAH: *(To JOY.)* Take her outside. I don't want her seeing this /

NORMA: *(To NOAH.)* I didn't know Maya was in the cupboard. /

HELEN: Maya? Tell your Daddy I'm Helen. She's Norma! Tell Daddy, please.

MAYA: You're a liar. Because you are a witch. Only a witch would do what you've done.

NOAH: *(To HELEN.)* Norma Pratt? You falsified your estimate and attempted to bribe a Utility Inspector in the course of his duties. Further, you have a broken ankle / and

HELEN: That's not true. It's a sprain. It's only a sprain.

> *NOAH kicks HELEN's sprained ankle and she collapses down into the recliner in agony.*

NOAH: You have a broken ankle. Maya is ruined. No amount of therapy can help her now.

HELEN: Please, I am not Norma. I know I said I am, but I'm not.

> *NOAH roughly slaps at HELEN's arm, looking for a vein.*

NOAH: By the power vested in me, I pronounce you officially worthless. You will now be cleared.

> *NOAH grabs his syringe. HELEN starts to struggle.*
>
> *NORMA squeezes her eyes shut and covers her ears.*

JOY: *(Shouting.)* Stop it! She is not Norma. She didn't know.

NORMA: Joy? It's me or her.

MAYA: Daddy. Is this a firm chat? Is this how you do burning? Did you do this to Ling May?

> *On hearing MAYA's voice, NOAH jumps away from HELEN.*

NOAH: *(To JOY.)* I told you to take the child out of this room.

MAYA: Daddy?

JOY: You got the wrong one. I'm Norma! Take me.

HELEN / NORMA: Joy!

NORMA: She doesn't know what she's saying.

JOY: I always tried to be quick. Kind. Make it painless. Happy chatting one moment, then gone. Like that. So quick. Never cruel. Never this.

NORMA: I promise you, Joy is not Norma. Because the truth is… I am Norma!

MAYA: I have meat faces in my head.

> *NOAH pushes JOY out of the way to get to MAYA.*

JOY: Daddy? Didn't you hear me?

> *NOAH looks from woman to woman, then turns his back on them and turns to MAYA.*

MAYA: They are all witches. They are all bad. Put them all in an oven.

NOAH: Don't look at them. They're fucking nothing. They're not you and me. Just ignore them.

MAYA: You used the fucking word again.

NOAH: I know. I'm sorry, darling. But it doesn't matter now… Just be quiet with me… I don't think I can do this any more.

NORMA: For God's sake, Daddy. Please grow a spine and get on with it. I'm ready, I've confessed and I don't see anything to be gained by drawing things out.

JOY: Silly old woman. Do you think I could let anything bad happen to you? Daddy? It was me!

NOAH: I don't care. You mean nothing now. Nothing. There is nothing. Look at her… Don't you see what you've all done to my baby?

> *HELEN, NORMA and JOY look at MAYA and MAYA just looks at NOAH and she is broken, and shaking. And the women see she is ruined. They grow quite and calm and sad.*

MAYA: Daddy? I feel… I think… I feel worse than when Ling May went.

NOAH: I know you do. I'm so sorry. This was not the plan I had in mind for today, sweetie.

MAYA: I want to go home.

NOAH: I know. I want that too. But… I don't think we can.

MAYA: I don't want to sit my test tomorrow. I don't have any fun things. I only have sad things in my head now. Can I do the test another day instead? Can you make them let me?

NOAH can't speak. He wipes his eyes, shakes his head.

MAYA: Why not. You're supposed to be good. You're supposed to be a good Daddy. Why did you let me come here? Why? Why do you let bad things happen. Why do you lie to me? You promised Mummy would be back. You said Ling May could stay forever. You lie. Do all grown ups lie? I want Dr Hardy. I want him. I can't feel a single nice thing.

NOAH: But darling, Dr Hardy couldn't fix what they have done to you.

MAYA: Then who will Daddy? Who will fix me?

NOAH: I've always tried to be a good Daddy, you know that?

MAYA: I want a safe-touch-time.

NOAH takes MAYA's hands and rubs them between his.

NOAH: Dr Hardy said you would always struggle to merit. But now this. You'll never pass. I can't afford to keep you if you don't merit. You'd bankrupt me.

MAYA pulls NOAH in to cuddle her.

NOAH: *(Cont'd.)* If you test tomorrow, the best you will ever achieve is a Comfort Girl. A Ling May for other people's daddies. I can't stand to see that Maya.

MAYA: It's OK. Ling May explained everything. When you have to do cock you just dream of clouds.

NOAH: *(Very gently.)* No more. No more of that talk, darling. It's time to be quiet now.

And now NOAH, very gently covers MAYA's, mouth and nose. Maya can't breathe. She starts to struggle.

NOAH: *(Very gently.)* Sleep darling. A prince is waiting at the other side… I'll never, never forget you. Shush.

NORMA, JOY and HELEN watch in horror as MAYA fades…

And then HELEN snaps, takes up the butchers knife that still lies on NORMA's table and slams it into NOAH's back.

NOAH, shocked, lets go of MAYA, staggers, hits out.

HELEN stabs him again and again and now blood begins to pour from his mouth. He buckles and falls to the floor.

HELEN drops the knife, goes to MAYA. MAYA pushes her away, exits the room and HELEN rushes to follow her.

Leaving NORMA and JOY, shocked, looking down at NOAH.

NOAH: *(Cont'd.)* Oh. Oh God. Help me.

NORMA: Joy. Don't just stand there. Get the polythene out. He's bleeding out all over my floor.

JOY gets the plastic while NORMA searches NOAH's pockets. She finds cash and pockets it.

Then JOY and NORMA roll him up into the plastic.

NOAH: *(Muffled.)* No. God. Please. Don't! Please? Help me…

JOY and NORMA watch as NOAH, rolled in plastic, quietens, twitches then stops moving.

Long shadows stretch until darkness falls…

SCENE 9 – GARDEN/HALL/LIVING ROOM – MORNING

SOUNDS of Seagulls calling, as sunlight returns.

NORMA in a dressing gown, sits in the recliner doing a crossword.

JOY scrubs at the bloodstained floor.

Meat sandwiches sit curling on the table from yesterday.

The SOUND of the doorbell.

NORMA: Joy? The door.

JOY: We can't have guests in when there's still blood on the carpet!

> *But before JOY can get up, HELEN, disheveled in yesterdays clothes, with her balaclava on, limps in from the Kitchen.*

> *HELEN peels her balaclava off and stands staring at them.*

JOY: *(Cont'd.)* Here's Helen! Come to see us Norma. What a nice surprise.

NORMA: *(To HELEN.)* Just because you have started murdering people, it does not make you immune to the norms of social convention. I would prefer it if you didn't just let yourself in.

HELEN: I thought I might as well. The door is open.

NORMA: It is not. It has been ripped from its hinges. There is a philosophical difference.

HELEN: If you say so Norma.

NORMA: I do say so. What do you want?

> *Silence… This is difficult for HELEN.*

HELEN: My ankle is bad. I wondered if I could have a bottle of the painkillers back?

> *NORMA thinks, then nods at JOY and JOY produces a bottle and hands it to HELEN.*

HELEN: Thank you.

> *Silence… HELEN can't take her eyes off the sandwiches.*

HELEN: And God help me, 'Little Helen' still needs to eat.

HELEN picks up a sandwich and devours it.

NORMA and JOY watch then join her in eating.

JOY: It gets easier, dear.

HELEN: I'm sure it does.

NORMA: Did Mr Brown take care of Daddy's van?

HELEN: He had it burnt out down Shady Lane. Though he says, without Daddy's body the Utility will still search high and low for him.

NORMA: We do not waste windfalls in this little home.

HELEN: So I've learnt.

JOY: I don't think we should talk about that, Norma. Not around Helen… Out of respect.

NORMA: Fine. But mark my words. We will all be glad of Daddy come winter.

HELEN: Maybe.

NORMA: Maybe, she says. Since Joy has retired from all wetwork involving children, understand this, eking out Daddy this winter will be our only hope.

JOY: I don't mind the curing or carving. Its the killing. I just can't face trying to kill another child. It always ends in such an awful mix up. No offence meant, Helen.

NORMA: You don't need to keep going over it Joy. /

HELEN: I meant… Maybe we'll have a different option by winter.

NORMA: How long do you think prize crosswords can survive, when new words get banned and redacted every week. No. The Sandwich Circle needs a reliable source of meat.

HELEN: You're misunderstanding me. There is a glut of Utility Inspectors in this town. Many are Incomers. There is no need for any of us to ever eat a child again.

NORMA and JOY put their sandwiches down in shock.

NORMA: Are you suggesting what I think you're suggesting?

HELEN: Yes I am. Because as it turns out? We all have the stomach for burning Utility Inspectors.

JOY: Helen! You'll regret this. You're too nice. Stop while you're ahead.

HELEN: You're wrong. I'm as surprised as you but I found it easy. And I could do it again.

JOY: Oh Helen!

HELEN: Think about it. We'd be killing two birds with one stone. And Mr Brown thinks, if we got really organised, we might build up a surplus. Imagine what we could do with that.

JOY: The woman I spied on for five years would never have said that. Never. That's just /

NORMA: Absolute genius… Do you know, Helen? I've always liked you. Deep down. Yes I have.

HELEN: *(To JOY.)* And I do think if Mrs Cooke were still able to have an opinion, she would approve.

JOY: Well I suppose? To be fair. No, you're right. Poor Mrs Cooke would approve.

NORMA: So, no more children. Utility Inspectors it is. And we'll do it for Mrs Cooke. Though I doubt we'll have a surplus. Not now we seem to have gained a child.

JOY: Norma. She's not a little girl any more. It's tomorrow. Everything has changed forever.

HELEN looks at NORMA, pointedly.

HELEN: It certainly has. Did Mr Brown fix your chair for you? I asked him to. /

JOY: Oh he did. And we're very grateful. Aren't we Norma?

NORMA: *(To HELEN.)* Yes. Yes. We're so very grateful to Helen… Just go and deal with Maya!

HELEN: You're welcome dear. Where is she?

NORMA: Still sulking in the Garden. She hasn't moved an inch since you left last night.

As MAYA is revealed, curled up around her balloon in the Garden, action in all locations becomes simultaneous.

HELEN: I'm not sure I'm the best person to get through to her Norma. Really, not after /

NORMA: Well she won't listen to Joy or me, so try. Otherwise she'll be all over the bloody / vine.

JOY: Vine… Oh she will be. And we can't have that.

HELEN starts to hobble towards the Hall door. But as she goes, she hands NORMA her 'legal' amber permit.

HELEN: I thought you might want this. See… You're legally 60 years old now dear. That makes you 10 years younger than me. I thought that might please you.

HELEN squeezes NORMA's hand then hobbles on. NORMA holds the amber permit, looks it over. Deeply moved.

NORMA: Helen. This is… Thank you!

HELEN smiles but doesn't stop to acknowledge NORMA, rather she keeps hobbling on, moving out of the Living Room and into the Hall.

Meanwhile as HELEN journeys toward the Garden, JOY finishes eating and NORMA gazes at her new permit.

And then HELEN steps into the Garden.

HELEN: Maya? You can't just lie here. We have to talk. /

MAYA: You said it was a game! You let me hide in that cupboard. You ruined everything.

HELEN: I didn't know what was in the cupboard. I didn't.

MAYA stands holding her balloon. She points a finger at HELEN.

MAYA: Bleep… Zuk-a-Zuk-a… Beep… Ffffffff… Beep…

In the Living Room, JOY goes back to scrubbing the floor, while NORMA pockets her new permit then picks up a crossword.

In the Garden, MAYA continues to point at HELEN.

HELEN: You're a young woman now. The time for games is over. It's time to face the truth.

MAYA: Truth? Here is truth. Your eyes right now are the same as Daddy's were, when he said he didn't burn Ling May!

In the Living Room NORMA looks around, frustrated.

NORMA: Joy! Have you seen where I put the *Chambers Dictionary*?

JOY: Helen took it home with her last night, remember?

In the Garden:

MAYA: Your face is the same as Dr Hardy's when he said I could merit if I really tried.

HELEN: Stop it.

MAYA: What's the word to describe Helen? It must be bad! I think it's liar.

HELEN: Stop it! Alright… You're right. I didn't ask or look because I didn't want to know / and

MAYA: Helen is a liar. I hate you.

HELEN: I'm sorry. I used you. That wasn't nice, Maya. But I am alive. And I'm not sorry about that. And I'm not sorry that I stopped your Daddy hurting you, because you are beautiful.

In the Living Room NORMA frustrated, slams her crossword down, hauls herself up and out to the Hall.

As soon as NORMA has exited, JOY slips into the armchair and she shuts her eyes and she clings onto the arms. Hard.

In the Garden:

HELEN: *(Cont'd.)* Try and understand. You're in the world now. Things are messy and wrong but /

MAYA: I'm not ready. I want my Daddy.

HELEN: It's Tomorrow. Coming, ready or not. You're all grown up. This is it.

MAYA: But I don't want this.

HELEN: I know. I don't either. But here we are.

> *HELEN reaches out to MAYA. MAYA pushes her away.*

MAYA: No.

HELEN: If you try, I'll try too. And I promise you I'll never lie to you again. Ever… Maya?

> *HELEN reaches out to MAYA. MAYA suddenly folds into HELEN's arms and they stand there, just hugging, while the balloon bobs gently above them.*

> *Until NORMA reaches the back door and pops her head out.*

NORMA: *(Shouting.)* 'Little child brings great sea change'? Six letters… Helen?

HELEN: For God's sake. Couldn't you please just give us one moment.

NORMA: We missed the post for all of Friday's closing dates.

HELEN: I know, but Maya needs /

NORMA: There's a secret puzzle going round the Vine. It's worth a kilo of lard. Mrs Solomon set it apparently. I've always liked her. Every answer an illegal word. We can win this, dear!

MAYA: It's El Nino… It is! 'Little child brings great sea change'? Six Letters. It's totally El Nino.

> *A surprised smile crosses NORMA's face.*

NORMA: Well now Helen, she might just earn her keep. Bring her in.

> *NORMA turns and shuffles back into the HALL.*

NORMA: *(Calling.)* JOY! Some fresh tea!

> *In the Living Room JOY leaps from the recliner. Straightens the antimacassar. Stops. Creases it again, then exits to the Kitchen.*

> *In the Garden:*

> *HELEN goes to the back door, turns and puts her hand out.*

> *MAYA hovers, then takes HELEN's hand and steps inside.*

THE END

By the same author

Ugly
9781849430210

WWW.OBERONBOOKS.COM

Follow us on www.twitter.com/@oberonbooks
& www.facebook.com/OberonBooksLondon

www.ingramcontent.com/pod-product-compliance
Ingram Content Group UK Ltd.
Pitfield, Milton Keynes, MK11 3LW, UK
UKHW031250020325
455689UK00008B/126